MW00609504

JUDY WILFORD

Judy works with the media of fabric and thread and the many and varied techniques of hand embroidery. Her unique embroideries draw on years of personal study and practice in design, drawing, painting, print-making, clay and object making; but it is the flexibility and technical variety inherent in textiles, in particular hand embroidery, that has and will continue to fascinate her.

Her works are held in diplomatic, corporate and private collections in Australia and internationally. She holds a Churchill Fellowship – studying ancient and contemporary narrative embroideries in the UK in 1999; a Diploma of Design from the Embroiderers' Guild, NSW Proficiency Certificate for Appliqué: Distinction; and is an accredited tutor with the Guild and TAFE (the leading provider of vocational education and training in Australia).

Judy is a well-regarded tutor throughout Australia and New Zealand at Textile Forums and McGregor Schools (University of Southern Queensland) tutoring her developed techniques revolving around birds and their habitats, the wider landscape and narrative works. She won the 2013 National Australian Society of Miniature Arts Awards for Mixed Media and the 2012 Yvonne Perring Memorial Award for best use of Traditional Techniques.

She has written articles for various magazines and books, such as *Masterworks* and *Inspirations*, as well as having her book *Embroidered Landscapes* published by Sally Milner Publishing.

embroidered birds
and their habitats

DEDICATION

I wish to dedicate this book to –
All the birds that sing.

embroidered birds
and their habitats

hand embroidery techniques and inspiration

Judy Wilford

SEARCH PRESS

First published in 2023

Search Press Limited
Wellwood, North Farm Road,
Tunbridge Wells, Kent TN2 3DR

Text copyright © Judy Wilford 2023
Photographs by David Elkins Photography and Mark Davison
at Search Press studios
Photographs and design copyright © Search Press Ltd. 2023

All rights reserved. No part of this book, text, photographs or
illustrations may be reproduced or transmitted in any form
or by any means by print, photoprint, microfilm, microfiche,
photocopier, video, internet or in any way known or as yet
unknown, or stored in a retrieval system, without written
permission obtained beforehand from Search Press.
Printed in China.

ISBN: 978-1-78221-766-4
ebook ISBN: 978-1-78126-724-0

Readers are permitted to reproduce any of the artworks in this
book for their personal use, or for the purpose of selling for
charity, free of charge and without the prior permission of the
Publishers. Any use of the artworks for commercial purposes
is not permitted without the prior permission of the Publishers.

The Publishers would like to thank Sally Milner Publishing
for their kind permission to reproduce the stitch diagrams on
pages 154–159.

The Publishers and author can accept no responsibility for
any consequences arising from the information, advice or
instructions given in this publication.

Suppliers
If you have difficulty in obtaining any of the materials and
equipment mentioned in this book, then please visit the
Search Press website for details of suppliers:
www.searchpress.com

Extra copies of the templates are available from
www.bookmarkedhub.com

ACKNOWLEDGEMENTS

When a book is written there are so many
to acknowledge and thank, such as those who
will publish the work, Search Press: Katie French,
Edward Ralph, Marrianne Miall and David Elkin
the photographer.

To my family and friends, many of whom do not stitch,
but have supported me at shows, exhibitions
and workshops through many years.
Thank-you.

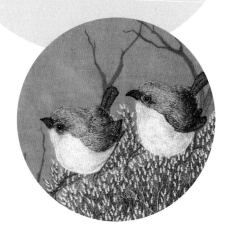

MIX
Paper | Supporting
responsible forestry
FSC® C012521
www.fsc.org

Contents

Introduction

The calls and songs of birds:

The carolling of a magpie

The piping call of the spinebill

The yodelling of a kookaburra.

The varied patterns and brilliant
colours of feathers:

The iridescence of a satin bower bird

The patterns of a curlew sand piper

The glory of a king parrot.

The adaptation of a bird to its habitat:

The webbed feet of the swan

The camouflage of the tawny frogmouth

The curved beak of a honeyeater.

The wonder of flight:

The tumbling acrobatics of the rose robin

The soaring flight of the wedge-tailed eagle

The gliding flight of the wandering albatross

The amazing migratory cross-Pacific flight of the
short-tailed shearwater.

Such is the fascination of birds.

Frosty Morning – Eastern Yellow Robin
30 x 40cm (11¾ x 15¾in)
Golden breasts glow
First call of a morning delights
A new day begins.

This book, of embroidered birds and habitats, expands on some of the enduring passions of my life: the arts, the land that surrounds me, and the celebration of a few of the birds I have observed and worked on over many years.

I lived most of my life in the Australian countryside, from the beaches of the southern coastline of my childhood, to the remote dry tropics of the East Kimberley. Now, after thirty-plus years of living perched over a ravine in the New England Region of New South Wales, I am a 'townie', living in the lovely city of Armidale of the same region.

My embroideries draw on many years of personal study and practice in design, drawing, paint, print, clay and object making. It is the flexibility and technical variety inherent in hand embroidery, however, that continues to inspire me.

I cannot remember a time when I was not investigating nature and art in all their many and varied forms; looking into the wider and more complex aspects of the land and the birds and animals that inhabit it. While I was nursing in the Kimberley region, an old bushman introduced me to the different ways of closely observing the many birds and their relationship to the landforms and flora of the region. His delight in small birds became and remains a constant thread in my life.

This book is the result of many years of personal research into the life of birds and their habitats, and also the results of ongoing experimentation and refining of my embroidery techniques. I wanted the works to reflect the translucency of a watercolour and contain the detail of low-relief textures found in nature. I also wanted the designs to be realistic, to reflect the beauty of both bird and habitat in a way to which the viewer could relate.

Living in remote areas of the country, with little access to books, let alone computers, had many advantages when developing my art. If you wanted to do or learn anything, you did it yourself. Such isolation, combined with a lack of direct influences and rules, allows one to develop a style and way of work that can become essentially and recognisably your own. For this reason, the way I approach the different processes in this book, such as design, is the way that I find works for me. It may not be the way you work, or as past artists may have done traditionally, but I hope you find them useful. In the spirit of developing your own style, I also encourage you to adapt all or part of them.

The way I work can be adapted and used by any embroiderer in any country in the world to produce works that reflect the birds and habitats of their regions. It is a fact that many habitats are replicated throughout the world, as are the birds that live in them. Where there is flora with nectar, there will be a form of honeyeater. Where there are flowers and leaves, there will be insects and a form of insect eater, and so on.

Birds are the most conspicuous of all creatures in our gardens, the woodlands and forests that surround us. As such, they are one of the most studied and feature symbolically in many emblems, cultures and religions – for example, the Dove of Peace, the Phoenix or the Thunderbird.

You need not be a scientist or an official 'twitcher' – a birdwatcher or a ticker of lists – to simply watch and study them, for the pure pleasure of doing so is one of the uplifting joys of life... as is embroidering a work of art.

Equipment and materials

When purchasing any materials or equipment, always choose the best you can afford. Cheap papers, inks, paints and dyes can – and often will – fade or deteriorate over time, particularly if exposed to light. Should you feel it necessary to save your designs and drawings for future reference, the manner in which they are stored is also important.

The materials and pieces of equipment listed are simply those that I use daily in one way or another. There is a constant flow of new products into the market, but I am sure that you also have particular tools or materials that you love to use. While experimentation is good, don't feel pressured to change for the sake of change.

Design and drawing

Pencils You will need graphite pencils from hard to soft in the following grades: 2H, HB, B, and 2B–6B. Coloured pencils, including watercolour pencils, will help when designing.

Pens I use fine line drawing pens, such as the Artline Drawing System or Uni-ball, and calligraphy pens. Be aware that some ink pens can fade under bright light. There is a wide range of coloured inks and dip pens with different nibs and inks. I also have a fountain pen, favouring Noodler's ink and a range of suited nibs.

Paint When I use paint, I use artists' quality acrylics or watercolours. I also sometimes use inks.

Brushes I use sizes from very fine 000 up to 5. As with paints, I recommend the best quality brushes. I find Golden Sable synthetics hold a point well, and are both cheaper and stronger than a true sable brush – a worthwhile consideration when using acrylics, as they can be tough on brushes. I also find soft, flat Japanese brushes and finely textured sea sponges useful.

Rulers You will need a variety of rulers. I use clear plastic and steel rulers in 15, 30, and 60cm (6, 12 and 24in) lengths. Attaching fine sandpaper to the back of the steel rulers will prevent them from slipping when cutting papers.

Papers Drawing or cartridge papers of varying weights and qualities are available in either sheet or block form. I use various sizes for design drafts, from large A2 (42 x 59cm/16½ x 23¼in) to smaller A4 (21 x 30cm/8¼ x 11¾in) layout or bank paper blocks. Blank page notebooks and visual diaries in various sizes are useful, as are office style card and tissue paper.

Others In addition to the main materials above, you will find the following invaluable: a set square, tape measure, erasers, a rotary knife and blades, a craft knife and clip-off blades, a self-healing cutting board, sticky tape, a light box, a camera, and a filing cabinet or other suitable storage system.

Pictured here are examples of my pens, paintbrushes, and pencils, along with accessories including a pencil sharpener and eraser, glue, craft knife, rulers and sticky tape.

Embroidery tools

From fabrics to threads, ribbons to suedes, and from fine leathers to beads, the choices of colour, weight, quality and brand names available to today's embroiderer is truly amazing. Choose carefully: using cheaper tools, or grades of threads and fabric which fade or degrade, will alter the quality and future value of your work.

Needles Crewel embroidery needles in nos. 9, 7 and 5 are the most versatile for the work. You should also have chenille needles in nos. 18–24, and some fine beading needles.

Scissors You will need paper, fabric and embroidery scissors – all sharp with long-pointed blades rather than short. Fiskars make beautiful spring-action scissors that are kinder than most to your hands. Never, ever lend them to anyone. It amazes me how many different, damaging ways some people find to use scissors.

Stiletto or awl These are sharp-pointed tools. You can use them either to make holes in the work, through which heavy textural threads can be eased ready for couching, or for manipulating the shanks of eyes for the birds.

Tweezers Fine pointed or curved tweezers can be used to help position you small sections of elements into place.

Forceps When you need additional grip for grasping and pulling needles through fabric layers and leathers, forceps are ideal.

Iron If possible, find an iron with a flat surface (i.e. no holes) plus a soft, stable ironing surface and a Teflon appliqué mat.

Frames Hoops and roller frames are not suitable for the main work because of the time taken to complete it. This, combined with the pressure used while stitching through layers, means that the tension is lost, to the detriment of the work. A rigid frame is therefore essential to the work, as it provides the best tensioning of the base fabric – and thus the work to follow.

Embroidery hoops These can be used to stitch the bird and other elements such as tree branches, which are to be applied at a later stage to the work.

Clamps C- or G-clamps, also known as fretsaw clamps, are essential. They are used to clamp the rigid frames to a table or a work stand. They must open wide enough to accommodate both the edge of the frame and the table. Leather, heavy card or felt pieces will protect table surfaces.

Extras The following are also useful: thimbles if you use them, tissue paper, clear sticky tape and a few pins). For the sake of completeness, you will need a clean ruler and 2H pencil for embroidery; though you can of course use the ones from the design and drawing materials on page 10).

Pins, needles, scissors, shears, tweezers and stiletto

A selection of threads

Threads

There is a vast range of brands and types of thread from which to choose. There are stranded cottons, perlé cottons, silk threads and ribbons of different types, not forgetting the unusual irregular threads, all of which can be space-dyed, over-dyed or hand-dyed. Many can be found from local and other needlework shops, by mail order or via many websites – try to make time to explore their wonders.

We all have our favourite threads that we use for traditional or other styles of embroidery. I mainly use DMC stranded cotton for their wide range and quality of their colour gradation. I find it a stronger thread with a better sheen than other brands. I also use silk threads and 2, 3 and 4mm silk ribbon for specific effects. Many of these I dye or over-dye myself, or source from other textile artists.

Softer, heavier threads are not suited to the work due to the difficulty of drawing them through the various layers. However, they can be couched into place on the surface of the work with a variety of stitches. I advise you not to use wool, as the thread is very prone to insect attack.

A strong thread will be necessary to lace stitching frames and backing boards for completed work. For this, I favour cotton tapestry warping threads such as Bockens Fishgarn 20/6.

Materials for finishing effects

An important part of the stitching process, these elements are never used simply to embellish the work, but form an integral part of it.

Found objects Shells can be stitched into sand ripples on a beach to help evoke and reflect the environment of the bird in your work. Found objects from other settings can also be used.

Beads Useful for adding texture and interest, these can be used to indicate the shine of sap in the bark of a tree, for example.

Teddy bear eyes Found at retailers selling products for making teddies. These typically range in size from 2–5mm (⅛–¼in), but larger eyes can also be found. Some have a curly wire or a looped wire on the back to stitch into place. The eyes I use for the smaller birds are 2mm with a shiny surface; they come in black or clear with a black pupil. The clear eyes can be painted with acrylic paint in whatever colour needed.

TIP

Clean found objects if possible, even if they come from jewellery. Shell necklaces, for example, collect old skin and body oils when they are worn. If not washed thoroughly, they will eventually mark the work. You would be surprised how dirty they really are!

Fabrics

The layering techniques that I use mean that you will be stitching through several layers and therefore the weight and weave of the fabrics used are important. Bear this in mind when choosing the fabrics to be used to form the background of the work.

The fabrics you use must be one hundred per cent natural fibre: cotton, silks and linen. Synthetic fabrics are not suitable as they tend to slip, and do not lie flat – they 'bubble' slightly between the layers. Like threads (see page 13), woollen fabrics attract insects and are best avoided. The fabrics must also be lightweight or mediumweight and relatively finely woven. Heavyweight, textured, and openweave fabrics do not lie flat under the silk organza overlay, which results in puckering, distortion and a degree of tearing along the stitched lines.

The background colours are chosen to match with and develop the design, so the fabrics must be of solid colours and have no discernible pattern. Patterns are distracting and detract from the surface stitchery to follow.

When you are on the 'hunt' for fabric for a project and you find something, get more than you need – you may never find it again! I always take a piece of white silk organza, the most often used overlay colour, with me when I'm 'hunting' to help test fabric combinations to be used for a background. The use of the organza layer will knock back the colour intensity of the background by approximately half, therefore it is better to check before you buy.

I have found it better not to launder the fabrics unless I am to colour them in some way as the stiffness from the sizing can be helpful when cutting various background elements.

Frequently-used fabrics

Listed below are the fabrics I use for layering the backgrounds of much of my work.

Cotton Most good-quality cottons up to and including homespun weight are suitable. Avoid mercerized cotton such as shirting, as in most cases the weave is tight, difficult to stitch and often reacts poorly with the silk organza. Avoid cheaper cottons as some are very stiff and full of dressing.

Silk Lightweight organza, lining silk (sometimes called Jap silk), and silk noile (a slightly textured raw silk sometimes called seedy silk) are all useful.

Felt I use lightweight wool and polyester blends; the polyester seems to help prevent insect attack.

Other The use of fine silk paper, made from silk tops or caps, and fine man-made suede and leather will be described in later chapters. Paper-backed fusible web is used to help prevent fraying; it is never used to fuse layers together. Polyester wadding (batting) is also used for padding birds.

Silk organza

Lining silk

Cotton

Storing fabric and thread

A closed, dark cupboard is better than open shelving, where fabric can collect dust and fade when light hits it; particularly on the folds. The best way of storing fabric is to roll it into a cylinder. Where rolling is not an option, such as for expensive silks, fabrics can be lightly folded between acid-free tissue paper. Fix extra shelving in a cupboard rather than storing fabrics in densely packed stacks or squashed into containers.

Regardless of the method you choose to store your fabrics, check them frequently for insect invasion because those little beasties just love munching their way through your favourites.

Keep silk ribbons loosely wrapped in small organza bags: those that come wrapped around cards are best ironed as soon as possible and stored in the same way.

Keep threads in their original hanks or spools. Don't wrap them around little bits of card as the thread becomes permanently creased and damaged – and it always seems to me to be an incredible waste of time. However, certain threads, such as silk bouclé or chenille, I wrap around a rolled and stitched cylinder of felt.

Jewels of the Forest – The Forest Kingfisher

39 x 39cm (15⅜ x 15⅜in)

These brilliant blue kingfishers are true gems of the heavily-treed swamplands and waterways of the forest ranging across much of the north and east areas of Australia. Once seen in their habitat they are never forgotten.

The work space

It is sometimes said that 'every man needs a shed'. In the interests of fairness, then, one can only presume that every woman deserves a studio!

Sadly, finding such a space is often not an option. Even after many years of working in the arts area, I still do not have the luxury of a purpose-built, dedicated studio – though happily I do have a room that is mine alone. In this room I store the ever-growing collection of fabric, thread, resources and books; it is here that I write, draw, paint and design and lay up frames.

Once prepared, I have the opportunity to work at my movable stitching cradle (pictured below) in any room of my home I wish. Other needs – such as a space for wet work, dyeing or airbrushing – can be worked around. I generally use the laundry for such tasks.

I find there are three essentials for a pleasing work area – a good light, a comfortable and adjustable chair and a suitable work table. However, don't wait for the room – get on with the stitching. That is what is really important. The longer one procrastinates, the lower the likelihood of achievement. One of my favourite quotes, shown to the right, comes from the German statesman and writer, Johann Wolfgang von Goethe (1749–1832).

'Whatever you can do, or dream you can do, begin it. Boldness has genius, power and magic in it. Begin it now.'

Stitching cradle

Combining a stable surface, storage drawer and foot rest for comfort, this stitching cradle was made for me by Chris Wilford.

The window

The 'window' is a tool that will be used through all steps of the work. While designing, it helps you with the accuracy of placement of the background layers. It will isolate the mounting allowance from the embroidery, which helps in maintaining perspective, and it also helps when mounting the work. I make windows to suit the size and format of every piece I make.

I use office card or cartridge paper for the window. Add 6cm (2¼in) to both the vertical and horizontal dimensions of the finished size, in order to give a border of 3cm (1⅛in) – this is the minimum mounting allowance necessary.

Using a steel ruler and knife on a cutting board, cut a central window giving a border of 3cm (1⅛in). Marking the centres and thirds on each side, as shown to the right, is helpful.

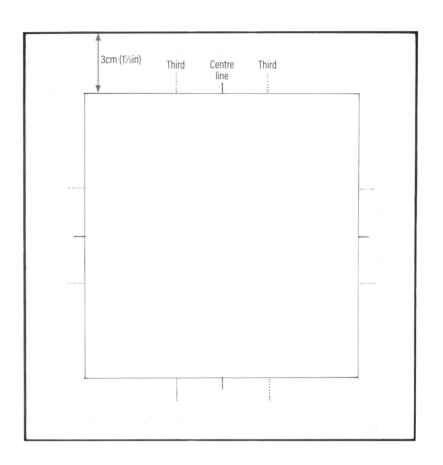

3cm (1⅛in)   Third   Centre line   Third

The Seed Eaters – Diamond Finches

36 x 24cm (14¼ x 9½in)

These bright, stocky, upright little grass finches are found mainly in the open grasslands of the Eastern States of Australia, and are quite different in attitude and shape to the slender genera of some grass finches.

The rigid frame

The rigid embroidery frame starts as a flat rectangular frame with fixed corners (see right). The frame must be level so that it will lie completely flat. The frame should have either glued or screwed lap joints and be smoothly sanded but not finished in any other way. Such a frame is very simple to make; any handyman or framer could make one for you, or you could try it yourself. Artists' stretcher frames can be used but do check that they lie flat and are stable.

The frame can be as long as will clamp to a table, but the most important measurement is that it should be no wider than double the measurement of your forearm from the wrist to your elbow. Working on these frames means that every stitch taken is a stab stitch: due to the tension of the work surface a slipped stitch is impossible. Therefore, doubling your forearm measurement means that, with practice, you can stitch from both sides, giving you complete control over your thread as you stitch.

There are many advantages to using these frames; depending on their size you may have several works on one frame at a time and, once correct, the tension will remain the same for all. For the projects later in the book, I suggest a frame size of 30 x 40cm (11¾ x 15¾in) internal measurements. It is a decent size to start with if you have not worked in this way before. It is also handy to have a smaller frame for stitch trials for your records.

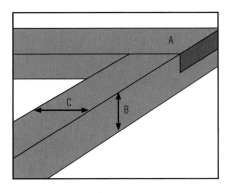

Corner strength

A lap joint is ideal for the corners of the frame (A), as it provides sufficient strength to avoid distortion. Mitre joints do not have sufficient strength. The frame should measure 1.5–2mm (¹⁄₁₆in) in depth (B), and 30–40mm (1¼–1½in) in width (C).

You will need

- 30 x 40cm (11¾ x 15¾in) frame
- Two C- or G-clamps – make sure they accommodate the frame and table depth
- Fabric and paper scissors
- Strong thread and a suitable pointed needle with an eye to take the thread
- Unwashed calico
- 40mm (1½in) masking tape
- H pencil
- Iron and ironing board or pad

Constructing the frame

1 Dampen the calico and cover it with an ironing cloth to prevent the size from scorching and sticking to the iron. With a dry hot iron, iron the fabric dry. This will shrink it slightly. Repeat this step several times until the calico has the feel of parchment.

2 Place the frame flat onto the prepared calico and draw around the outside edge with a pencil. Cut away any excess with the fabric scissors.

3 Fix the calico to the frame with masking tape: start by taping the corners to the frame, positioning the calico precisely. Next, tape the long edges and then the short sides. Keep tension on the calico while taping.

4 Clamp the frame to the table with one long edge protruding beyond the edge of the table, calico-side up.

5 Stitch the calico to the frame using a large buttonhole or blanket stitch. Begin by pulling the thread through the fabric at the corner of one long side (if you are right-handed it will be the left corner of the frame), then tie it tightly around the frame leaving a 'tail' of 10cm (4in).

6 Hold the thread to form a loop to the right of the tied stitch. Insert the needle into the top of the calico next to the frame, pull it through and bring it up through the loop at the outside edge of the frame. Pull the thread through tightly and continue stitching in this manner towards the left-hand corner. Use your left hand to maintain the tension on the thread with each stitch as you work.

Blanket stitch   Tie-off-point

Masking tape

Calico

Front of the frame

7 Hold the tensioned thread to the left on the outer edge of the frame and finish with a stitch through the top of the last stitch and repeat. This is similar to a half hitch knot and will lock the stitched line into place. Leave a tail of 10cm (4in) and cut.

8 Unclamp and turn the frame around (180º), reclamp and stitch the opposing long side in the same manner, this time inserting the needle 0.5–1cm (³⁄₁₆–³⁄₈in) from the inner edge of the frame into the calico and pulling the thread firmly against the inside of the frame to tension the calico. To finish, tie and clip off as before.

9 Stitch the two short sides in the same way.

10 To tension the corners, tie the 'tails' together at each corner on the outside of the frame and clip off close to the knot.

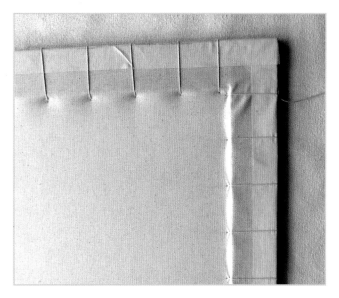

These details show the front (above) and back (below) of the tensioned frame.

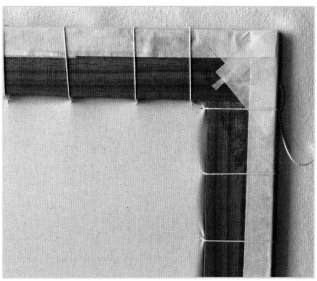

TIP

Unwashed calico is used as the ground for the work because it contains sizing, giving it the necessary stiffness.

Maintaining tension

If the tension is maintained throughout stitching, the finished frame will be drum-tight. If the tension is lost while stitching, it will be difficult to regain. Try adjusting the tension at each stitch. If this is not successful, the side will need to be restitched.

The length of thread for a frame will be approximately four times the full length of the side being stitched.

I have found that the distance between the stitches directly relates to the width of the wood used to make the frame. Therefore, if the width of the wood is 3–4cm (1⅛–1½in), then the distance between the stitches will be approximately the same. This distance between stitches is also useful when maintaining stitch tension because, if the frame is closely stitched, it is almost impossible to maintain a good tension.

Should you run out of thread while stitching a side, finish off in the same way that you would at a corner and start again in the same way you began. When the side is completed, tie the thread ends together and clip to maintain tension at the join.

Resource and research

The preferred habitat of the bird we choose to embroider is very important. Indeed, it is my belief that the bird and its habitat are of equal importance, and you really do have to get both right. It is not good enough to place a bird specific to the rainforests on desert flora because you like the colour combination. It might look great, but someone out there is going to tell you that you have got it wrong – usually loudly and publicly! You do not need to be a scientist, but you do need to research your subject area and you need to develop and to use your powers of observation to ensure that the relationship between the bird and its habitat is accurate.

Then, for our purposes at least, so long as you keep the bird and the habitat in its context, you can lift a bird from one resource and place it in another more suited to your embroidery needs – and the process of designing your work will have begun.

Birds and habitat

As with all creatures – ourselves included – birds have certain fundamental requirements. Water, food and shelter are the most important, and must come from their environment. Therefore, the accessibility of water, and the nature of the local vegetation and landscape often influence the birds in a particular environment – be it the coastland or waterway, forest or desert. It is interesting to note that wherever habitats merge, one finds the richest source of bird life.

Different bird families may occupy the same habitat and territories, but their requirements are not necessarily the same. As they have differing needs, some species can co-habit in that environment peacefully. The magpie, for example, is very happy alongside restless flycatchers or finches. Such species thrive on the edge of open forests and woodlands overlooking the open spaces of grasslands. Enter the choughs or the currawongs, however, and the magpie will 'declare war', as these birds compete for the same resources.

Related bird species may be widely distributed throughout a continent. A good example can be found with the Australian fairy wrens, which occupy every terrestrial habitat in Australia, from forests and swamps to deserts and grasslands. The fairy wrens are insect eaters in the main, but will take seed and berries. They rarely drink, and forage mainly in the shrubby undergrowth of the lower canopies of open woodland and dense grass clumps, all bordering small open areas. Therefore, the adaptable small, beautiful fairy wrens find their niche pretty well everywhere.

On the other hand, some birds have very specific needs and will only occupy a small specific habitat. The wonderful palm cockatoo is found exclusively in Cape York Peninsula, while the tiny mistletoe bird exists only where there is mistletoe – if all mistletoe was to be destroyed through clearing or fire, this bird would quickly become extinct.

Some birds form a territory within a habitat and remain there for life. Others, such as the dollar bird, are nomadic. Following the seasons, these birds crisscross the country from Victoria to the Kimberley and into New Guinea. Some birds are known as altitude nomads and travel up and down from the coast to the Tablelands Region of Eastern Australia and back. The shy yellow-faced honeyeater is a good example of a seasonally-influenced nomad.

A collage of habitats

A showcase of the sheer variety of places in which birds thrive: everywhere from the coast and waterways to the forests and woodlands, the tablelands and slopes, and the plains and deserts.

Birds across the world

We find birds that are the same or similar in many different countries. Often when a 'new' country was settled, old common names were adopted for native birds. The robin is one such example. Some say it is simply nostalgia for the settler's former country that drives this, but possibly it is because of the bird's place in the wider landscape or habitat and the attitude of the particular bird that allows the naming.

Other birds that fill similar habitats in many countries are the kingfishers, finches, warblers, fantails, bell birds, rock wrens and the silvereye. Parrots and parakeets, spoonbills, herons and egrets are further examples. Amongst the water birds are various shags, terns, and albatrosses.

We tend to become very parochial about our own countries but the birds fill the specific roles of honeyeaters, insect eaters, seed and fruit eaters, night birds, water birds and waders in all countries. Likewise, local birds of prey like the eagles and songbirds such as warblers are found in every country, and everywhere their roles interlock with their habitats.

Scientific classification

Classifying birds is a way of understanding the diversity of the thousands of distinct species throughout the world. The classification of a single species follows these steps:

Class – Order – Family – Genera – Species – Race

The best way to understand the principles of classification is to use a specific bird as an example:

The red-browed finch

The red-browed finch, our subject for the project on pages 56–99, lies within the Aves class because, like all other birds, it has feathers. It is this that distinguishes birds from other animals.

Our red-browed finch ranges in a broad band from the Cape York Peninsula along the Great Eastern Ranges through Victoria into Adelaide. At this time, it has no known races or sub-species.

Class Aves

Order Passeriformes (perching or songbirds)

Family Ploceidae (weavers, grass finches and allies)

Genus *Neochmia* (grass finch)

Species *N. temporalis* (a description of specific characteristics – in this case, the colour of the finch's brow)

Races Nil.

Finding resources

There is an abundance of resource material available for both birds and their habitats. Books, magazines, calendars and cards have many photographic, painted or drawn examples. These are available through various retail outlets, regional information centres, libraries and museums. They can also easily be found online. It is worth noting that much of this imagery will be under copyright and, as such, you must seek permission from the copyright holder, and acknowledge the use of the original image if your resulting work is to feature in the public arena in any way.

Sometimes, if you make an appointment with museums or universities, you can view or even borrow study skins of birds in much the same way as you can borrow a book from a library. Detailed measurements and feather patterning can be obtained from such skins. If you do use study skins, it is important to keep in mind that the bills, bare skin areas, legs, and claws often lose colour on death, due to the cessation of blood flow.

Besides these external sources, however, I find that personal observations, writings and sketches are often of much more use to you, the artist, than any other resource. It is these personal observations that will make a work 'live' by capturing, in word or line, a bird's attitude and behaviour – and they will do so more effectively than copying directly from a book.

Keeping a visual diary

Drawing is perhaps the most important skill available to the artist, regardless of the area of the arts in which they work. It is also one of the more attainable skills as it is the simple result of observation and the practice of hand–eye skills. Most of us attain the skill of writing text – some better than others, admittedly – and drawing can be thought of as an adaptation of writing.

Try maintaining a visual diary, drawing for half an hour every day for six months. Use a mix of different pencil and pens, and draw anything you see: don't waste time setting up the perfect still life. Instead, draw the used teabag on the bench as well as the flower in the garden or the fungi on a log. In fact, take your sketchbook with you everywhere you go. After six months you will have attained the skills needed for drawing; it is then a simple matter of using them to keep in practice and to develop your work.

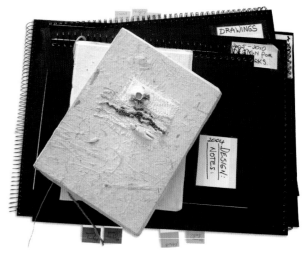

A selection of my sketchbooks. Some are store bought, but another hobby of mine is book making – sketchbooks are a perfect excuse to combine my interests.

Natural treasures

Birds are a product of the landscape they inhabit. Elements of the landscape, such as the items shown here, can help to inform our understanding of the bird. Drawing the seeds, shells, leaves and similar objects that relate to the bird's habitat is a perfect way to practise. They are no less important than the birds in your artwork, and just as deserving of study and sketching.

24

Nest with Eaglet

Spinebill's Woven Nest

Using and storing your reference

For my artwork, I use a combination of drawn and written observations of both bird and habitat. I take photographs of the wider view of the habitat as well as close-ups of various features that may be useful. This is valuable because I can use this information to produce several works. Photography is wonderful for reference because of the camera's ability to capture the wonderful sense of movement and freedom that is, to me, the very essence of the bird. Just remember that a photograph's colour is not true, due to several factors, ranging from light, to development and printing.

It is important to have a couple of good reference sources to help verify your observations. I use the *Field Guide to the Birds of Australia*, published by HarperCollins, which I find invaluable for the bird naming and official colour identification. Having said that, your description of a bird's colour may well differ from the 'official' colour. Everyone perceives and describes colour slightly differently – how many different ways would you describe 'ginger' or a 'citrus wash', for example? – so I suggest that you primarily rely upon the colours you see in a bird for your artwork.

Your resource and research material is a valuable and re-useable commodity. Keep it. Keep all of it: photographs; drawings both rough and detailed; your colour notation and descriptions of birds, flora, and elements of the land such as logs, rocky outcrops, pebbles, leaf litter; as well as images of the wider landscape. You never know when they may be useful. General observations and notes of seasonal changes to the land and behavioural changes in the birds should be kept. Some behaviours you will see each year and some observations you may never make again.

Stay organized

Work out a system of filing and storage that allows easy access to your resource material. Photographs and clippings from magazines and similar sources can become part of your collection, too.

Remember to note details of publications, artists or authors wherever possible: you may need at some future point to acknowledge or request permission to use their work.

Drawing birds

'How do you draw birds? They don't stay still long enough to put pen to paper.' This common statement has some bearing in truth. Birds, particularly small birds, are wonderfully active and attempts to draw them can often lead to frustration. Drawing birds requires patience and much practice but, more importantly, it is an awareness of their actions and acute observation of their behaviour that will lead to success.

Where to start

In the comfort of your home, begin looking through some of that resource material you have collected; at paintings and photographs of birds. Study these images and look for the basic shapes inherent in a bird's body. Think of the old childhood riddle: 'What came first, the chicken or the egg?'

The bird comes from the egg and it retains this simple, compact shape all its life. Birds differ in many ways; there may be a long neck or a fanned tail, but the basic egg shapes of body and head remain in all. When you can see these shapes within, you are ready to begin.

Take a soft pencil and with tracing paper over the image, find and lightly draw the egg shape within the bird's body, then find the egg shape within the head and impose that over the body. Try this simple exercise with as many images as possible and you will see that a simple egg shape for the body, with a smaller egg shape, the head, slightly overlapping the first gives you the basic shape of a bird. If you can visualize these two shapes when studying birds live, you will find it helpful with your drawings.

Working freehand on paper, practise drawing these shapes in varying positions until you are confident with them.

Capturing posture

Many field sketches are very rough, giving only an indication of position and poses. Acquired memory and word sketches can fill out visual observation, so what these roughs should aim to capture is the movement and the essence of the bird. It is this sense of life gained in the field that will cross over into the more accurate drawings you will need for your design and ultimately your work.

The bird's shape and the position of the head will express its behaviour and attitude. A resting bird is more rounded, its head nestled into the body and the body settled and 'fluffed' around its claws. In contrast, an alert bird's head is up, the neck extended, the body upright on tensed legs ready for flight.

The more you observe birds, the more aware you will become of how behaviour and attitude changes their basic shape. Practice drawing the underlying shapes (see opposite, top) roughly and quickly, at different angles and sizes, while maintaining the head and body at approximate proportions of 1:3. You will soon see that only slight adjustments of the head will relate to the bird's position and attitude.

It is now time to find and place the basic details of the bird. Most field guidebooks will have a diagram or map of the parts of a birds' body and wing patterning, and this will be an invaluable source of information.

Sketchbook studies

Each of these studies captures the basic details of the bird in question: head, overall body shapes and important details.

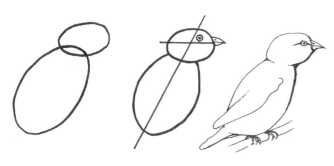

From basic shapes to attitude and posture

Examples of obtaining movement and attitude. Note the overlapping egg shapes of the head and body in each example.

The head Its main features are the bill and the eye. If you draw a horizontal line through the middle of the head extending outwards in the direction that the bird is facing, you will have the position of the bill – examples of this are shown above. This line is the division of the upper and lower sections of the bill. The eye always falls above this line within the first quarter of the bill side of the head.

The ear coverts will further divide the head into the crown or cap and the chin from the neck and the nape. The coverts are small feathers that cover the bases of larger ones or feather masses, e.g. wing coverts.

Body shape Draw a vertical line dividing the shape equally, extending the line to indicate the tail. Viewed side-on, the wings separate the back and the rump of the bird from the breast, flank and abdomen. The wing will fit approximately into the upper half of the divided shape. Following the line, the tail folds away under the central or largest feather of the folded wing. Viewed frontally, the vertical line through both head and body shows the features of both sides to be equal. Slight changes will alter the position of wings and tails accordingly. The tail can be fanned out, raised and flicked as needed; wings can be opened as in flight.

Apart from wings and tails, the other part of the body that changes a bird's attitude is the neck. Apart from the obvious difference in length between species (compare a swan to a scrub-wren), birds' necks have a wide range of movement and flexibility because, unlike our necks, their heads turn on one pivot. Because of this, you can expect a bird's head to assume many postures – angled, extended and contracted – not seen in other vertebrates.

Details With your egg shapes in the right attitudes or positions, and the outline of the bird in place along with the bill, eyes, wings and tail, it is now time, with the help of your observations and resource material, to ascertain the type of bill, claw, tail length and colour areas that accurately describe your bird.

Taking Flight – Red-browed Firetail Finches

60 x 24cm (23½ x 9½in)

A series of sketches of an old distorted mallee in a water-gouged gulley combined with the addition of a small flock of finches and the basis of the work was formed.

This work is based on the use of diagonal lines that give tension to the work and a sense of movement and flight to the birds. Note that the open lattice-work of the branches follows the placement of the birds, allowing the eye to travel through and around the work from the upper left towards the lower right. This is also mirrored with the lie of the land, the grass and flower bank.

Design

'Design is not the offspring of idle fancy; it is the
studied result of accumulated observation.'

So said master designer John Ruskin (1819–1900), and nothing could
better describe the designing of a work based on the subject of birds
and their habitats.

As with drawing, designing needs practice and an understanding
of the processes taken to produce a workable design. We understand
what we can see; the tangible qualities of line, shape, texture, value and
colour, known as the elements of design. However, it is the intangible
qualities, those we cannot see, inherent in the principles of design
such as balance, contrast, repetition, movement and unity that bind
the elements together and it is here that difficulties can arise. Of these
qualities, balance is probably the most important.

Balance is described as 'the equality of elements and principles within
a design'. Obtaining this balance is essential to the success of the work.

Our aim is to obtain a balance between the dominant subject,
the bird, and the secondary subject, its habitat, each being of equal
importance to the other in a real sense as well as a design sense.

There are many approaches to developing a design. It is my personal
approach that I will be describing throughout this book. Some of
you will work in other ways, but this works for me. If elements of my
approach appeal, then feel free to include them in your design process –
and if you find that the approach as a whole works for you, I invite you
to use it.

Line

To me, line is the most important of all the elements of design. In particular, lines describe the landscape. Just consider range or hill lines, tree lines and grass lines, plough lines, fence lines, water and tidal lines and many more. Design without line is impossible.

Lines can be made by pencils, pens, brush and needles using graphite, ink, paint and stitch.

Lines may be continuous or broken, sharp or soft, thick or thin, apart or close.

Lines may be straight or wavy; jagged or flowing; and can create movement or rhythm, aggression or harmony.

Lines may be purely directional or used to suggest an emotional aspect: vertical lines are static; horizontal lines are calming; curving lines give movement; and diagonal lines create tension.

Lines create tone or value, they define or enclose; creating shape and form, pattern and texture.

Lines converge and cross, forming divisions in space, perspective and focal points; and they make edges, forming planes.

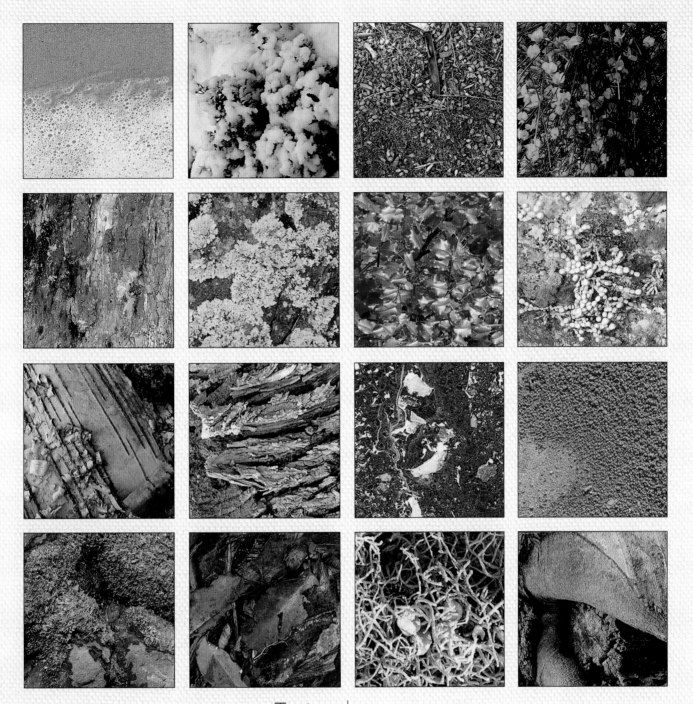

Texture

After line, I find texture to be the second most important element. As line describes shape, texture describes the quality of a surface, be it actual or imaginary.

Actual texture is that which can be felt: smoothness or roughness; a glass surface against lichen on a rock. Imagined texture is created by the artist using various tools and a combination of elements – line, marks or tiny shapes - to describe an object. Texture arranged in an orderly or formalized manner becomes a pattern.

The essence of texture is manifold:
The smoothness of river pebbles: the polished surface of water and glass. The reflective sheen of metal; the slick of oil on water.
The bubbling surface of foam; the granular sensation of sand between toes. The roughness of sawn wood; the curled fragments that pattern the floor. The gossamer threads of a spider's web; the patterns of fish and snake scales.
The coarse, broken bark of ironwood; the smooth gleam of leaves ruffled with wind.
The random scatter of daisies in a field.

Colour

'If you, unknowingly, are able to
create a masterpiece in colour, then
un-knowledge is your way. But if you are
unable to create a masterpiece in colour out
of your un-knowledge, then you ought to
look for knowledge.'

Johannes Itten, *The Art of Colour*, 1973.

Colour may be the most complex of all elements of design. At root,
however, the theory of colour is based on the principle of contrast.

There are many design books available which will describe
all elements and colour theory in detail, complete with exercises
and the use of varied materials in all art and craft genres. It is
interesting to work through colour exercises, but it is not until you
put the theory into practice and adapt it to your subject area that
you understand what you need to produce a design from which
you can work.

As my work is based on a realistic and impressionistic
interpretation of the land and nature, I allow my observation of
their colour changes to inform my choices. Take time to observe
the colour around you, be it a park across the road, the landscapes
of your region, your workplace surroundings or the places you visit
on vacations. The colours in a landscape are directly influenced by
day-to-day – and season-to-season – changes.

Record in some way such changes: the change from clear,
bright light to dull when clouds move across the sky; the
differences between colours at sunset and sunrise, or from winter
to summer. These are a few of many.

DESIGN

The Nestlings – Scarlet Robins

32 x 40cm (12½ x 15¾in)

*This design is based on a combination of diagonal lines that lead into, and direct the eye
towards, an enclosed space. The muted green-grey hand-dyed and painted fabrics suggest
the quiet and stillness of the surrounding habitat, while the lines of the major branches upon
which the birds perch direct the eye to the nest and its contents. The dull colours of the nest and
shrubbery are indicative of a secret or hidden place. These dull colours enhance the contrasting
colours of the flame robins.*

The design space

The design space is also known as the format. For our purposes, the design space is essentially two-dimensional, in that it is to be viewed from a single direction. Layered work such as collages or embroideries are considered two-dimensional, but may also be referred to as low-relief.

The design space contains the dynamics that affect the balance of the visual elements placed within giving impact to the work. There are several ways to use the space to obtain the balance needed within the composition or design:

Rule of thirds   This well-known example involves dividing the design space into three, both horizontally and vertically. The result is a grid of thirds, where the intersections become the focal points. Working this way will reliably lead to a balanced design.

Odd numbers   The so-called 'rule of odds' involves the placement of an odd number of elements – usually one, three or five – within a work. Even numbers create stability, so odd numbers tend to create more active and interesting compositions – though not always.

Designing landscapes and nature for an intended work often involves the art of rearranging and adapting the elements seen in the real world into a balanced composition suitable for both the composition and, importantly, the techniques to be used. Therefore, I suggest that you work within the guidelines or rules but, if your observations of the bird and its habitat demand change, do not hesitate to break the rules and do it.

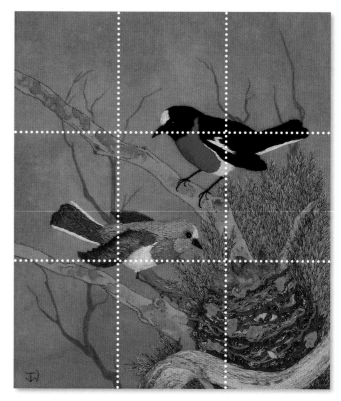

Rule of thirds

The intersections of the dividing lines make good spaces for a focal point, or points. Here, the two adult birds are placed on two of the intersections, while the mouths of the nestlings are on a third, at the bottom right. It is interesting to note that a focal point need not have an actual visual element. It can instead be an empty space, where the eye rests after moving through the work.

34

DESIGN

Design: towards obtaining a balance

There are several ways of treating the design space that are particularly suited to birds in their habitats. The examples opposite show some examples.

Central or near-central   Placing the principal element, the birds, at the precise centre of the design space is powerful but also static. The placing of an element off- or near-centre controls attention by creating tension and movement between other elements.

Left versus right   In the West, works tend to be 'read' from left to right. If there is a visible barrier at the left-hand edge of the work, the design will have a sense of heaviness, an immobility that the design must overcome for the rest of the work to be properly read or experienced. Work that does not have a visual barrier, but instead an openness, allows the eye to travel easily though the work.

Curved line

A curved line within a square or vertical space embraces central to near-central subjects. Here, the birds and their perch are those subjects, the curved line resulting in a sense of repose and harmony. However, alertness and movement can be emphasized by the direction the head and bill faces. Further tension and movement can be added with the placement of the habitat's features.

Enclosing lines

An enclosed design, particularly with a squared format, gives a sense of secrecy, intimacy and safety. Behaviour and alertness, suggested by head direction, will offer movement. This style of composition is particularly suited to nesting, where the placement of the subjects' shapes will draw the eye to the focal point and around the subject matter.

Diagonal lines

Diagonal lines within a rectangular design space will give tension to the design, enhancing a sense of movement and alertness. With this approach, placing the birds on either the right- or left-hand side does not matter greatly: depending on the position and attitude, the birds will appear to sense danger and be ready for flight. The repetition of diagonal lines within the habitat, foreground and background will emphasize the forward-looking movement of the birds. This composition is well-suited to the edge of a woodland into an open landscape type of habitat.

Choosing a bird and habitat

For a first work, I recommend choosing a small bird, such as a wren, a finch, a robin or a spinebill, from your sketches and research. I also suggest you avoid one with intricate feather patterns such as a quail, sand piper or a parrot; opt for one with distinct colour changes.

- Decide on the number of birds you want to include in the work and make sure both sexes are shown, as they often display variation in colour.
- Once the bird has been chosen, consider the broad habitats where the bird is found. For example, the forest and edges, the fields, the deserts, the beaches and/or the urban areas.
- Decide on the primary features to be used – those that will relate directly with the bird, a log, branches, boulders, nests and flora. These will become part of the foreground features.
- Next, decide on the secondary or distant features – range lines, hill and tree lines and grass lines. These will become part of the middle and background features.

An overview of creating the working design

Visualize how many birds you want to include, and their placement in their habitat. From observation and research, I often build a story based on the birds' activities – perhaps hunting, flying from undergrowth, courting or bathing, nesting or feeding the young fledging. I then decide on the shape and size of the design space.

1 When creating a working design, I start with a line drawing of my chosen bird; a cartoon drawn up to the size and format to suit the proposed embroidery. Keep in mind that the aim is not to create a detailed drawing but a working design. As such, it must show clearly the lines to be transferred from paper to fabric.

2 Next, draw the birds up separately and in relative detail. Their individual shapes can then be traced onto black card, cut out and arranged. Using silhouettes like this means that you can quite easily adjust their position across the background, either individually or in a group.

3 Once you have completed your design, create a master copy by drawing it out clearly and neatly using a fineliner pen on cartridge paper. This ensures you have a clean, clear version to refer back to at any stage.

4 Once the master copy is complete, you can create additional layout copies that focus on particular parts of the design, such as the background layers. You can also use it to plan the surface stitching; which elements will be worked on-frame, and which off-frame.

The following pages look at some examples of how I have approached different working designs, to show you how the basic approach above can be applied in practice.

Initial drawings and master copy

These were used to plan The Fledgling Superb Blue Fairy Wren *on the facing page. Proper planning is essential.*

The Fledgling Superb Blue Fairy Wren

15 x 15cm (6 x 6in)

*I saw this bundle of fluff on a boulder from a window in the house;
It was unusual for it to be in the open – particularly as the nest was in a
bush nearby and it was alone. It wasn't long before the female returned
from feeding, and moved the little one back into the bush.*

White-browed Scrubwren

These birds are small, active insect-eaters with a particular enjoyment of aphids. They flit and hop through rocky gullies and shrubbery in groups 'ts-ching' and calling to each other.

The background design for this work (see page 41) is based on the diagonal fall of the tree and rocklines of a gorge where I often sighted these wrens. These became the secondary elements of the design. The primary elements were the perches and the birds themselves. The shrubbery, grevillea, is marked with a dotted line on the design and acts as a joining element to bring all the elements of the composition together.

Important terms

These closely-related terms are used in the later projects, so make sure that you are familiar with them.

Master copy The master copy is a line drawing showing clearly all the lines and features to be transferred to fabric and stitch.

Layout copy Layout copies are traced from the master copy, and show particular areas, including allowances. Usually you will need one for the background fabric layers. Depending on the complexity of the proposed work, you might also need layout copies of the middle and foreground work.

Together, the master and layout copies make up the working design. All numbering and notation is made on the layout copies as needed.

Field sketches

As mentioned on page 26, field sketches need give only an indication of position and pose. As long as you capture the essence of the bird, a working drawing can be developed using your research and experience alongside the advice here. Colour notes, like those shown here, can be made on the spot or afterwards.

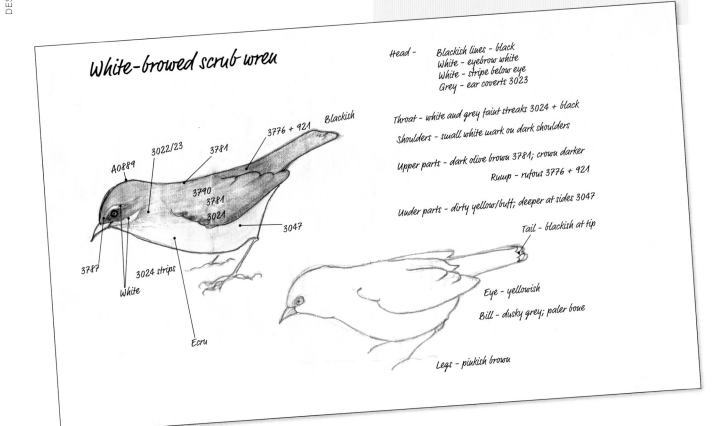

White-browed scrub wren

3776 + 921   Blackish

3022/23   3781

A0889

3790
3781
3021

3047

3787   3024 strips

White

Ecru

Head – 	Blackish lines - black
	White - eyebrow white
	White - stripe below eye
	Grey - ear coverts 3023

Throat - white and grey faint streaks 3024 + black

Shoulders - small white mark on dark shoulders

Upper parts - dark olive brown 3781; crown darker

	Rump - rufous 3776 + 921

Under parts - dirty yellow/buff; deeper at sides 3047

	Tail - blackish at tip

Eye - yellowish

Bill - dusky grey; paler bone

Legs - pinkish brown

Initial drawings

Based on the field sketches, these early drawings are useful because they allow me to explore the particular poses I want in my final design, but they need further development before they will be useful as a working design.

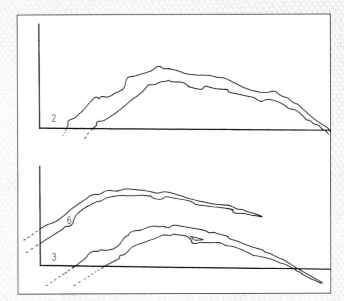

Card silhouettes and perches

It is important to determine the size and shape of the design space early on. Drawing out foreground details like these branches (right) will help you to experiment with the placement of the birds within their habitat.

Using the initial drawings as a guide, cut-out silhouettes allow me to easily arrange and adjust the position of the birds within the design. Note that the silhouettes only include the bulk of the body, not the legs. This is because there's no need to go into such detail yet – the final position of the legs will depend on where the individual bird sits within the design.

Line drawing

Once you are happy with the arrangement, a line drawing that combines the branches and birds in the correct positions can be made.

This line drawing includes major details like the eyes, legs and branches, as well as the positions of the tails and wings. These are clearly marked, to make it practical to use later, if you need to refer back to it.

Master copy

Time to put the birds in context. The master copy combines and develops the line drawing, adding more detail to the birds and establishing them clearly within their habitat.

Here I have suggested both the rocks and shrubs of their natural environment, and built this into the design using the notes on pages 34–35. For example, both the shrubbery and the rocks create diagonal lines that run from top left to lower right.

DESIGN

Layers

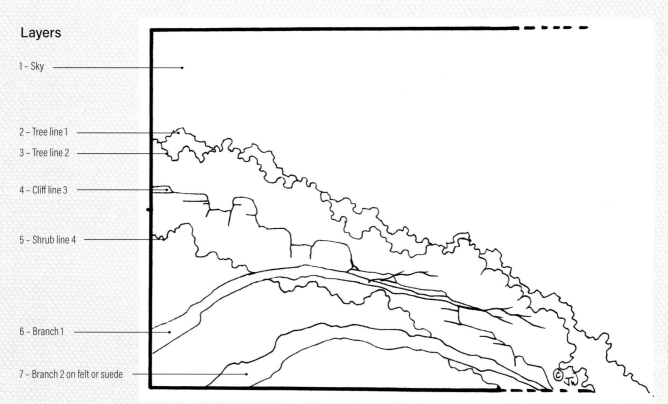

1 – Sky

2 – Tree line 1

3 – Tree line 2

4 – Cliff line 3

5 – Shrub line 4

6 – Branch 1

7 – Branch 2 on felt or suede

Additional layout copies

With the master copy complete, you can use it to further break down your design. This particular design needs a layout copy that details the background fabric layers, including the branches.

Some designs will require other layout copies that help to clarify the on- or off-frame stitching.

There was no need to do a separate on-frame surface stitchery layout for this work because there is only a single embroidered layer – the shrubbery.

On Alert – White-browed Scrubwren

24 x 16cm (9½ x 6¼in)

The shrubbery shown here is a grevillea. It encroaches onto the cliff face and over the branches. There is a line of distant trees following the cliff face edge.

The three wrens were stitched off-frame. Each was stitched individually on a hoop, and, when finished, applied to the work.

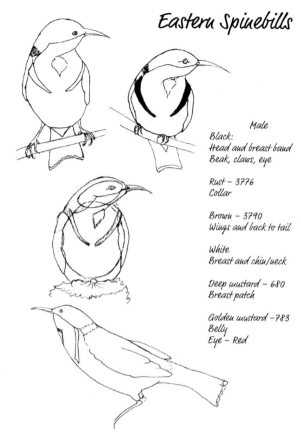

Male

Black:
Head and breast band
Beak, claws, eye

Rust – 3776
Collar

Brown – 3790
Wings and back to tail

White
Breast and chin/neck

Deep mustard – 680
Breast patch

Golden mustard –783
Belly
Eye – Red

Eastern Spinebills

This honeyeater enjoys nectar, particularly that of grevillea and bottlebrush flowers – so I wanted to make sure to include both in my design. As you can see in the initial drawings to the right, early on I explored a different posing option for the birds. On consideration, I felt the frontal view of the birds better suited the square format of the proposed work, while the direction of the birds' heads allows a sense of alertness and distance.

Being a simple design there was no need to trace up layout copies. The main drawing became the master copy, and this was all that was needed. The only time the working copies are traced up is for work involving the backgrounds of complex designs.

Initital drawings/sketches

DESIGN

The master copy

The master copy helped me to work out the order of stitching for the surface stitchery. On-frame, after back stitching the perch, I worked the branches of the bottlebrush, followed by the flowers, stems, leaves and then nuts.

For the off-frame surface stitchery, the birds were stitched individually on a hoop, then applied to the background (see pages 94–95 for the technique).

Eastern Spinebills

15 x 15cm (6 x 6in)

*Apart from the sky layer and branch, there were no other underlayers to the background,
and therefore only the branch was back stitched.*

Fine bare branches were painted onto the sky before layering.

*The leaves were cut out of painted suede and applied by back stitch as the central vein.
Some overlap the edge, throwing a shadow once mounted.*

Superb Blue Fairy Wren

Perky and active, these wrens are just one of several races. Insect-eaters, they work from ground level up into the lower storeys of the forest and shrubbery.

I love watching them. This is one of eight or more works I have made of these wrens. Almost all are based on a diagonal design plan; some have a layered background and some are of a single layer either spray brushed, sponged or hand-dyed. The one shown here is layered – as are the two projects later in the book.

DESIGN

Initial sketch

Line drawing and silhouettes

Master copy

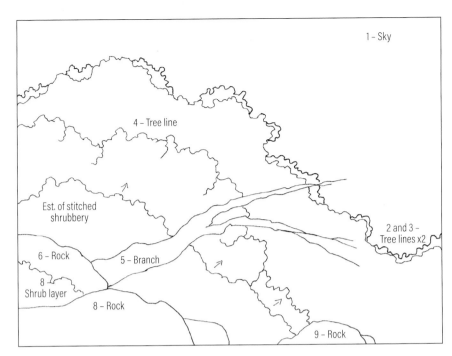

Layout copy 1

This layout copy shows how I broke down the background fabric layers including the branches.

Labels in the diagram:
1 – Sky
4 – Tree line
Est. of stitched shrubbery
2 and 3 – Tree lines x2
6 – Rock
5 – Branch
8 – Shrub layer
8 – Rock
9 – Rock

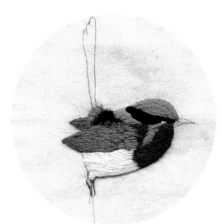

Off-frame surface stitchery

The two fairy wrens were stitched separately on a hoop and then applied to the completed background (see pages 94–95).

Superb Blue Fairy Wren

25 x 20cm (9¾ x 8in)

It's worth noting that your design work can be re-used to try out different ideas. The finished work above was the second based on the original master copy. The first work's shrubbery was a rosy heath myrtle (one of the baeckeas); but in this later version, tree line 3 has not been layered, and the shrubbery stitch line has been extended into the area. The placement of the rocks is also slightly different to the plan.

Drawing up a working design from photographs

You can draw up a design based on a photograph in much the same way as from your own sketches. However, they are not a shortcut. Although you have a photograph, it is still important to spend the time to research the bird and its habitats. Remember that both are of equal importance to the work.

The photograph you have chosen to use will often contain detail that is not only confusing to the eye but downright off-putting to the mind. Thus begins the 'gentle art of re-arranging': drawing up a design that is suited to your requirements and, importantly, the embroidery techniques. The photograph shows a split second, with particular lighting, and so the colour of the bird may not be that as described officially. Many photographs are taken in a closed habitat and you may wish to change it to a wider one.

If the photograph is not yours, always check on the copyright.

DESIGN

1 Start by examining the photograph and decide what you want to retain, and what you need to emphasize. Is the bird part of a wider landscape or part of a more intimate setting? Are there other dominant features, such as a hollow log, a mate, a nest, or shrubbery? Here, for example, the adult Caspian tern (on the right) is about to feed the juvenile – but the distance is too great to make an effective design.

2 Take a couple of black and white photocopies of the photograph. On the first, outline the details you want to keep in ink. If you decide to change the habitat's background, you can use the other photocopy. Outline the birds and adjust the background using a thick pen and block in the changes. Put the photograph away at this stage.

3 Start to refine the design by drawing an area of the same size. In it rearrange or reposition the different features by adding or deleting details until you obtain a balanced line drawing. You may need to alter the shape of the format or design space. With this complete, decide on the size of the proposed work and enlarge or reduce the design. If necessary, make up a window (see page 17). Does this design retain the essence of what attracted you? Adjust if necessary.

4 On a sheet of cartridge paper, draw up the design space and surround, then trace and ink in all the details needed for your master copy. You can then work the design up into a master copy as described on page 36.

The end result

Comparing the designs (left) to the original photograph, you can see how I removed the large rock and brought the two birds together; placing the adult in a more dominant position. I also changed the herbage into a seaside shrub, as I felt the stalky nature of the herbage was too difficult to represent in stitch. I did not use either rough for a work.

Challenge yourself

The most difficult bird I have ever stitched was the pygmy goose (*Nettapus pulchellus*) of Northern Australia. This small beautiful goose had the most interesting emerald green, grey and white chevron patterning that extended from its throat through to the undertail. A definite challenge!

From photograph...

...to planning through sketches...

...to the finished embroidery.

Choosing colours

With the master copy of your design to hand, we next decide on the colours of fabrics and threads to be used. If necessary, consult your reference material – your photographs and notes – and indicate these colours on a layout copy.

Choosing fabric colours

As noted on page 14, fabrics for backgrounds are best kept plain, in block colours. Tonal sponged and dyed surfaces, however, can and do work well. *Sipping Nectar – The Eastern Spinebill* on page 139, is a good example of a sponged surface.

Laying silk organza over a fabric will knock back the colour intensity of the underlying fabric, which allows you to create subtle colour effects. This is important to know when sourcing fabrics for a work. Choose colours of medium intensity as the white silk organza overlay will lower the intensity of most colours (see below) and will appear black if they are too dark. Therefore, check each fabric against those next to it, and the effect the organza has on all, and change if necessary.

Overlaying

The image above shows the uncovered fabrics, while the image below shows the softening effect of white organza on the fabrics. This is what helps to add subtlety to the work.

TIP

Different silk organza colours will affect the colour of underlying fabrics differently.

Choosing thread colours

Below are shown the threads used for the superb blue fairy wren (you can see the plan on pages 44–45).
When choosing threads for the birds it is a good idea to consult official ornithological colour notes. Compare them with your own observed notes and check the colours against a thread chart of your preferred embroidery threads.

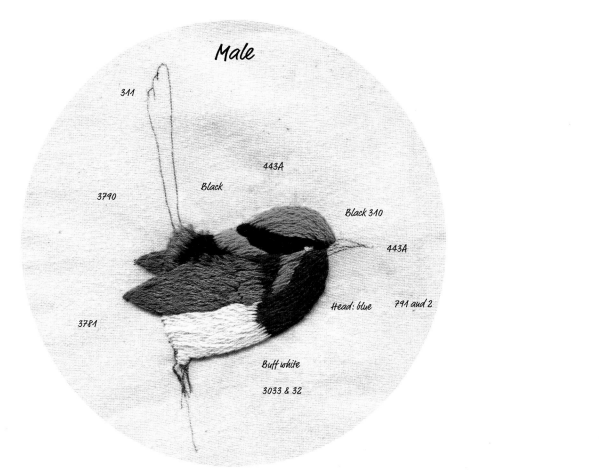

Male

311

443A

Black

3790

Black 310

443A

Head: blue   791 and 2

3781

Buff white

3033 & 32

Serenade – Grey Shrike Thrush

57.5 x 42cm (23½ x 16½in)

*The first call of the morning
The grey shrike thrush sings
A new day begins.*

The background is of sky-blue homespun cotton, airbrushed with the palest pink and the branches painted with acrylic paint. The forward limbs are cut out of suede and were sponged with a grey acrylic and, after being layered into position under silk organza, were back stitched. The colour range was kept to the subtle greys of an early sunrise.

The birds and the branch were stitched off-frame and applied. The female is placed in a lower position within an enclosing section of the branch while the male appears to dominate on the higher curve. The placement of the two birds caused much comment on the part of several guests at the exhibition opening where this work was displayed – and it was among the first to sell.

The order of work

This part of the book gives you a general overview of how to approach your artwork, and introduces some of the key ideas or processes necessary for all projects, such as layering and surface stitching. Use the information here as a practical starting point to help develop your designs into successful finished artworks.

Having an order of working gives your project structure. Note, however, that there is more than one approach to embroidery – indeed, when you come to create your own pieces, adapting your approach to better reflect the individual bird or its environment is important. The two projects later in the book (see page 56–99 and 100–119) therefore show how I tailor the general design, layering and stitching processes to the specifics of the piece.

Planning a work

At this point, you have a master copy of the design along with any necessary layout copies of the background fabric. Having chosen the bird and its habitat, and prepared your working design, you will already have formed some ideas of the fabrics and colours that could be used. Because the work involves a combination of embroidery techniques it is helpful to devise a working plan.

The work falls into two main areas: the fabric layers forming the background and the surface stitchery. It is further divided into that which is worked on-frame and that which is worked off-frame. It is the combination of both on-frame and off-frame work that gives a sense of distance, depth and dimension to the finished artwork.

I have written up a working plan for most of my works. Once you have devised a working plan and refined it over time, you will find that it becomes an almost automatic way of working.

On-frame work The underlayers incorporates the back, middle and foreground fabric layers, and all features or elements of the habitat that will fall under a layer of silk organza. These layers are numbered consecutively, from the top of the work to the base, on a layout copy. Any other features are also numbered. The organza completely covers the design space and all mounting allowances, holding the fabric layers in place until they are back stitched to secure them.

Once back stitching is completed, the surface work is done. Surface work includes the midground of trees and shrubbery along with the foreground stitching of grass and flora, and other details such as lichen on rocks.

Off-frame work Some elements of the design can be stitched on a separate embroidery hoop, and subsequently attached to the on-frame work. Such off-frame work typically includes hand-stitched birds, small and large branches, or tree trunks; and machine-constructed elements such as leaves, boulders, logs and petals.

Selecting fabrics

Next, we select the fabrics to be used. If necessary, consult your reference material – your photographs and notes – and indicate these colours on your layout copy.

Fabric weight As described earlier, choose relatively lightweight, closely-woven fabrics: homespun being the heaviest and silk organza the lightest.

Natural or synthetic? Choose natural fibres such as silks and cottons wherever possible – synthetics do not lie flat, often slip and are hard to stitch.

Background fabrics Using coloured silk organza as a background layer, such as a range line, will help to add distance to the work. As an overlay, it can give wonderful effects to the work, changing the mood and atmosphere completely. The colour you choose (see page 48) will give you options: a rosy pink can offer a sunrise; terracotta a dust storm; and a bluey-gray a rainy day. Two layers of differing colours will give another effect, so feel free to experiment.

Overlays Choose colours of medium intensity as the white silk organza overlay will lower the intensity of most colours and if too dark, will appear black. Therefore, check each fabric against those others that will be used in your project, and the effect the organza has on all and change if necessary.

This shows a selection of fabrics chosen for a project. On the right, silk organza has been overlaid to show how this affects the intensity of the colours. It's useful to test all the colours together.

Preparing the layers

Once you have chosen your fabrics, you need to prepare them for use within your design as follows, with reference to the layout copy and the window tool: prepare, cut and layer each fabric in order before you begin. Cut or tear all fabric layers into strips the width of the intended work, including the side mounting allowances. Strips should typically be cut or torn on the grain of the fabric. They can be laid onto the base fabric at any angle. Iron all of the strips making sure they are crease-free.

As there are no seam allowances, each fabric layer is traced and cut to its upper profile (for example the hill lines of a background). Each layer must be of sufficient depth to accommodate the following layer on the design. It is the 'underlap' of each layer of fabric that gives depth to the work, enhancing the low-relief effect. Therefore, measure from the highest point of the profile of a layer to the lowest, plus 3mm (⅛in) 'underlap' to accommodate the following layer. Usually the grass layers are torn and frayed to 3mm (⅛in) and are 3–4cm (1⅛–1½in) deep.

The first fabric used (usually the sky) must also include a mounting allowance at the top, as does the last layer forming the base or the foreground.

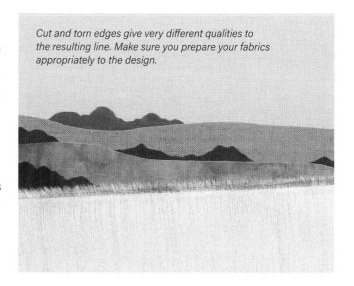

Cut and torn edges give very different qualities to the resulting line. Make sure you prepare your fabrics appropriately to the design.

Back stitching

Back stitching is an essential part of the work. It both holds the fabric layers in place and gives depth, dimension and a sense of distance to the work. It is done within the area defined by the isolation stitches (see page 69).

The stitch outlines the layer being stitched. It should look as if you have taken a pencil and drawn around the very edge of a shape or line. The only time a layer being outlined is stitched into is either to lock it into place so that it will not pull away when further stitching is done, or to define a detail such as the indentations of a tree line or a line drawn on the design.

A line or shape that is back stitched appears to advance towards the viewer while one that is not recedes. Because each layer is superimposed on the previous one, they will begin to develop a visual sense of low relief, giving depth and distance to the work.

Note that there are two forms of back stitching in both projects: one is stitching the layers (see page 71 for an example), and the other is stitching the elements such as branches (see page 72). The layers are stitched first, then the elements. When it comes to stitching an element upon which a bird is perched, then the back stitch and placement are worked together.

Stab and slip: stitching on- and off-frame

Every stab stitch will be taken in two distinct movements – up and down. This is quite different to those taken on the hoop or hand-held, which are called slip-stitches.

All on-frame surface work is made as a stab stitch. Most off-frame work is made as a slip stitch. This is because the tension of the base fabric on the frame must be drum-tight. If you can make a slipped stitch on a frame where the tension is slack, the fabric layers of the background will move and pucker.

Back stitching is always worked on-frame with this work, never off-frame. Working on a clamped frame gives you complete control over the needle, thread and stitch as well as the direction that you stitch. Every back stitch should be small, approximately 1mm in length, and must be even.

Back stitching is visible here around the branches, worked through the overlay.

Back stitch technique

Stitching always begins at the lowest cut fabric layer. This is most often a tree layer, but not always – it could be in the foreground, for example. The layers are then stitched one at a time towards the top of the work following the steps detailed here.

1 Begin with a small knot and work from the centre of this layer to the isolating stitch (see page 69). Take 3–4 stitches into the mounting allowance, ending with a tiny stitch into the last stitch.

2 Pull the thread through in the allowance or calico and clip off. Do not make another stitch as it will have to be removed.

3 Return to the centre and stitch towards the other side in the same manner. Working in this way for the first layer will smooth out any puckering that can occur, due to the slight movement of the fabrics, to the edges.

4 Continue to stitch each line in order from whichever side you prefer.

A stitch diagram is given on page 154.

Surface stitchery

Surface stitchery is the most exciting and creative, not to mention time-consuming, part of the work. Surface work includes all surface stitchery and all the stitched elements applied over the silk organza overlay. Just as the background fabrics are layered to create a sense of dimensionality, so the surface stitchery gives further depth to the work.

Once the back stitching is completed, the design is checked, and the stitching of the middle ground can begin. The elements of this area are usually trees and shrubbery stitched in a diminishing scale.

When planning and designing, be aware that the placement of the trees can (and often does) change while stitching, generally because slight changes occur during the cutting, layering and back stitching. This is normal and is a result of the natural movement of fabric against fabric. It also adds to the individuality of the work.

All surface stitchery must be completed before the birds are applied. After the birds are in place, return and complete any gaps in the flora to the edge of the bird. Never place the heavier stitching of flowers beneath the position you will apply a bird (see page 72), as the grass and shrubbery structure may run slightly under the tacked placement.

TIP

Unsure of a stitch? There is a stitch glossary at the back of the book that covers all of the stitch techniques used in this book.

Surface stitchery order of work

Whatever the project, surface stitching the work should proceed in the following way:

- From the top of the work – to the middle ground – to the foreground.
- From the centre of the work out to the sides.
- From the surface of the work up into relief.

Planning the work with these general rules helps to prevent the stitched areas from being excessively rubbed by hand or thread and helps to smooth out any puckering or distortion.

Detail from Courting Colours

The surface stitching here was done after the back stitching of the perches was completed. For the shrubbery I used adapted feather stitch (see page 77) to cover the designed area with a basic structure. I added the flowers using various arrangements of detached chain stitches, concentrated on the tips and intersections of the structure's stitches. Once all the flowers were complete, I 'slotted in' the leaves between the stitched flowers using the same stitch.

Other surface stitching here includes the legs and claws of the fairy wrens – mainly worked off-frame, these surface stitches were added once the birds had been stitched into place.

Finishing the work

Once all the birds have been stitched into place, it is time to finish off any last elements – typically flowers and leaves on shrubbery – and the work is completed.

After this, I place the 'window' into position over the finished work and put it in a place where I can see or catch glimpses of it during the day. I find this a particularly helpful way to ensure there is nothing else needing to be done on the work.

This stage also includes mounting and framing to present your work to best effect. This is detailed on pages 142–147.

Dawn Light – Superb Blue Fairy Wren Fledglings
38 x 29cm (15 x 11½in)

I have made several works based on these small, enchanting babes. I had plenty of opportunity to observe them from a window in my home where they emerged from their nest and stayed within the comfort and reach of it for a week or two.

The background is a single layer of hand-dyed cotton upon which branches have been painted using acrylic paints. The tree trunk and perch branch are suede. All have been back stitched with small branchlets and other details added. Note, however, that if one of the painted branches had not been back stitched, it would appear to be further in the distance than the others.

Once the branches and branchlets were complete, the flora was stitched and, on completion, the birds applied to the work.

The plan for this artwork can be found on pages 132–133.

Project One
A Brief Flash of Red

The red-browed firetail finch – *Neochmia temporalis*

PLANNING THE BIRD AND HABITAT

I have chosen for this project one of the beautiful Australian grass finches, sometimes known as firetails. Found in flocks that consist of several monogamous pairs, they inhabit open grasslands close to dense shrubbery and grass clumps and the edges of open woodlands near permanent water.

The similarities between this species and finches found elsewhere in the world (see below) is part of the reason I have chosen this bird and its related habitats for this project: the ubiquity of finches means that the body shape and environment will likely be familiar to you, wherever you live.

Should you wish to later change the subject to a local finch in a similar habitat, it would be relatively easy to do so – and my hope is that you will work many more of your own later. However, as this project is designed to introduce you to the techniques, I suggest that you start out by working each bird as designed.

The bird

Class Aves

Order Passeriformes (perching or songbirds)

Family Ploceidae (weavers and allies)

Genus *Neochmia*

Species *N. temporalis*

True finches, also called Old World finches, are found across various habitats of the northern hemisphere. Some have migrated and settled in Australia, while others have been introduced. The differences between these finches and the Australian finches like the red-browed finch are slight, limited to subtle differences in tail shape and length, and their colorations. However, the bill of both groups is strong, stout and pointed: that of a seed-eater.

The completed work.

CREATING THE WORKING DESIGN

Following the procedure explained in the previous chapter, I created a working design. In creating my work plan, I decided to design this work along diagonal lines, to give a sense of a flock moving from shrubbery into the grassland beyond.

Roughs and mock-up

I started with a line drawing; a cartoon drawn up to the size and format to suit the proposed embroidery. Keep in mind that the aim is not to create a detailed drawing but a working design. As such, it must show clearly the lines to be transferred from paper to fabric.

Although the bird always becomes the dominant feature of the work for this project, I worked on the equally-important background habitat first (see right).

Once I was content with the bird line drawings (see below), I traced the individual shapes onto black card and cut them out, before arranging them to form a flock. To give the design the sense of movement I wanted, they too were aligned in the diagonal (see opposite).

Habitat

The habitat I have chosen is based on sketches of a nearby landscape in New England, part of the New South Wales state of Australia. It is a simple design, in which the hills are seen as overlapping planes or lines interspersed with small groups of trees. Some are layered into the background, a surface stitched group in the midground and a foreground of stitched grasses and shrubbery.

58

PROJECT ONE

Design elements

Not all of these elements made it into the final design – only the branch at the bottom is used in the final design, for example.

The birds

As the most important part of the design, the birds were drawn up separately and in relative detail.

Card silhouettes

See page 39 for how these are used.

Master and layout copies

Once the placement of both habitat and birds was drawn up and balanced, I made a master copy of all layers and a layout copy of the background layers alone.

Master copy

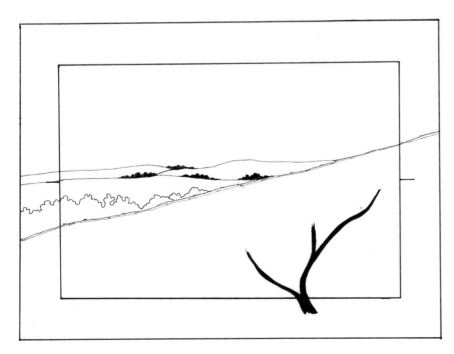

Layout copy

Here, the mounting allowance (see page 60) has been added to the design space. The master copy fits within the smaller rectangle, but the background layers of the design are extended to the full width of the layout copy, including the mounting allowances.

LAYERING THE BACKGROUND

Fabric preparation

Using the layout copy below and the window tool, prepare, cut and layer each fabric in order before you begin. After preparing the individual strips according to the notes opposite, lay them in order from the top to the base of the work.

Do not cut or fray any layer at this point – just gather the fabrics you need and keep them close to hand. It's best to do any preparation on a layer just before you add it to the piece in the next stage. Check, then turn them over together so that they are in the order to be laid.

Samples of the fabrics used in this project. Time spent early on choosing appropriate colours and fabrics that all work well together will ensure a strong, cohesive finished piece.

Layout copy noted with the order of layering

The design space holding the master copy measures 25 x 17cm (9⅞ x 6¾in). The mounting allowance in all dimensions is 3cm (1⅛in). The total size is 31 x 23cm (12¼ x 9in).

Mounting allowance

Fabric preparation sheet

This gives the sizes of all layers used in the layout, and any additional preparation required for each. The background layers must include all necessary allowances.

Fabric	Layer	Preparation
	1 – Sky	-Sky blue cotton, 31.5 x 15cm (12½ x 6in) -Iron
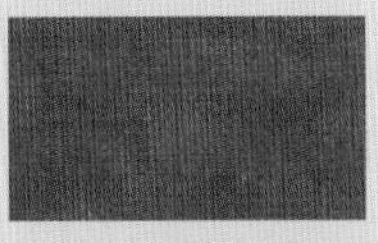	2 – Tree line 1	-Dark green silk organza, 4 x 4cm (1½ x 1½in) -Cut freehand (see page 64)
	3 – Hill line 1	-Mid-green cotton, 31.5 x 5cm (12½ x 2in) -Vliesofix (see page 63) with tracing (see box, right)
	4 – Tree line 2	-Dark green silk organza, 20 x 4cm (8 x 1½in) -Cut freehand and into sections
	5 – Hill line 2	-Mid-green cotton, 31.5 x 8cm (12½ x 3in) -Vliesofix with tracing
	6 – Tree line 3	-Dark green silk organza, 20 x 6cm (8 x 2⅜in) -Cut freehand
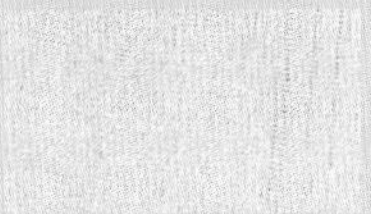	7 – Grass line 1	-Cream Jap silk, 31.5 x 4cm (12½ x 1½in) -Tear and fray (see page 65) 3mm (⅛in)
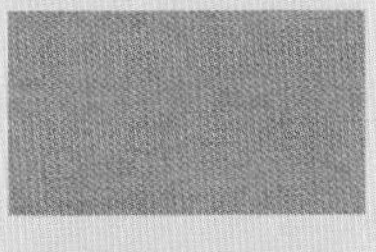	8 – Foreground	-Mid-green cotton, 33 x 16cm (13 x 6¼in) -Tear and fray 3mm (⅛in); mark, cut to fit sides and base allowances
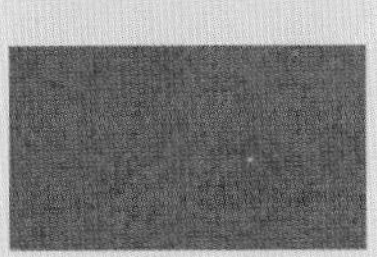	9 – Branches	-Brown suede, 6 x 12cm (2⅜ x 4¾in) -Trace, tape, cut
	10 – Overlay	-White silk organza, 31.5 x 23cm (12½ x 9in)

Tissue paper tracings

- Tissue paper is used to make accurate tracings of the design lines. The tissue is cut to the same depth, including mounting allowances, of all the fabric layers. Place the tissue over the design line to be traced so that the line falls to the top of a horizontal edge.

- Make the tracing with a fine ink pen. Should the line disappear under another layer, indicate it with a dotted line for a cutting guide. Trace each individual line on a separate tissue strip and note the line number or name on each.

- Pin the tracing to the 'right' side of the layer, making sure that the traced line lies over a Vliesofixed edge. To avoid marks, pin the tracing to the layer in the mounting allowances. The layer is now ready to cut when layering commences.

- Further background details such as rocks, logs or branches – particularly those relating to the bird – are also traced onto tissue extending into the mounting allowance as needed. Rather than pinning the tracing, use tape to fix it to the fabric and carefully cut around the traced line.

Layer placement

Place the prepared frame on the worktable and position the window tool centrally on the calico. Pull it forward on the frame so that the outer edge of the base of the window is resting on the internal edge of the frame. This central placement is important in maintaining an equal tension when stitching.

Refer to page 61 for a list of the layers.

You will need

- The prepared fabrics and tissue tracings ready to cut or fray and layer
- Rigid frame and clamps – laced and ready
- Window tool
- Scissors
- Pins
- Tweezers
- Small ruler

The window tool in place on the calico.

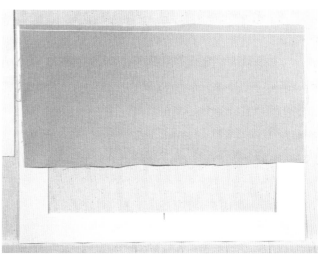

1 Pick up layer 1 (sky) and place it over the window so that all allowances are covered, as shown. Next, carefully remove the window, then replace it in position over the sky layer; there should be a sliver of the sky fabric at the top and side edges of the fabric showing (see below). From this point on, all following layers are superimposed upon the previous layer.

2 Layers 2 and 3 – tree line 1 and hill line 1 – can be laid together. This is because of the small size of the tree line (see above left) which is easily tucked into place under the hill. Above right is shown hill line 1, prepared with a Vliesofix strip (see box opposite) and pinned together with a tissue tracing in the mounting allowance.

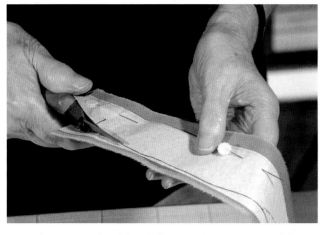 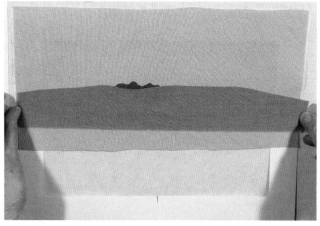

3 Cut along the traced line (above left), remove the paper backing of the Vliesofix from layer 3 (hill line 1), then position it over the sky layer. Check the position against the design and tuck the tree line into place, using the ruler if necessary.

After this step, if the placement of both is right, carefully remove the window, which need not be used again until the foreground layer and when putting the branches into place for the final check.

Vliesofix fusible web

Vliesofix is a lightweight paperbacked heat-reactive adhesive/fusible web used to adhere fabrics together or to prevent fraying. With this work it is only used to prevent fraying unless otherwise indicated. Because of this, only narrow strips of 1–2cm (⅜–¾in) are ironed on the top edge of the long or horizontal fabric strip. The side with the fusible web on becomes the 'wrong' side of the fabric.

- Fusible web is ironed only onto the cotton layers; never onto silk organza as the adhesive will bleed through the silk. Don't apply it to an edge that is to be frayed, because you will be unable to fray any fabric through an adhesive.

- To apply fusible web, use a dry iron at a temperature suited to the fabric and the adhesive. Place the Vliesofix paper side up and rough (adhesive) side down onto the fabric and press for 5–10 seconds. Allow to cool, then lift the paper end to check. If the adhesive has melted onto the fabric correctly, it will have a clear, shiny appearance. The paper can be removed when needed. If the fabric has an opaque web-like appearance, it will need to be ironed again at a slightly higher temperature.

TIPS

Other types of fusible web are available, but I favour Vliesofix because it is lightweight and easier to stitch through than others.

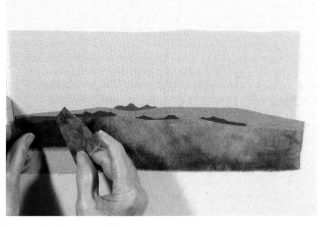

4 Layers 4 and 5 (tree line 2 and hill 2) are laid in a similar manner. The tree line is cut freehand as one section and then divided into three. The hill line is cut and laid in the same way as hill line 1 and its placement checked. Starting from the left side of the layer and working across, tuck each tree section into place by gently lifting the hill line from the right, altering the ends of each tree section as necessary. Be guided by the design, but at the same time be aware that cutting tree lines freehand is not an exact science.

5 Layer 6 (tree line 3) is cut freehand. Layer it in place over the base of the hill as shown.

Cutting complex lines freehand

Some lines, such as tree lines, are too complex to cut from a tracing and should be done freehand. You are trying to achieve a line that is irregular both in height and spacing. This technique is used on both silk organza and Vliesofixed layers. If it is a Vliesofixed edge, remove the paper beforehand: if left in place after layering, the layer will buckle as it is back stitched. To cut, hold the Vliesofixed edge uppermost.

1 To start, put the end of the fabric into the open 'jaws' of the scissors. Rather than cutting the fabric as usual, instead gently move it backwards and forwards as you slowly close the blades of the scissors.

2 When the scissors cease cutting, open the blades. Move the fabric back into position, then continue cutting and manipulating the fabric as described above, until you reach the end of the layer.

3 Place the layer onto a flat, contrasting surface and check the cut line. Should it resemble even V shapes, you have cut too quickly; if it looks like even scallops, too slowly. If it appears too regulated, the fabric has been cut as if in a straight line. In all cases, cut back into the line and remove small sections. The result will be a beautiful complex line resembling tree canopies.

6 Layer 7 (grass line 1) has been frayed by 3mm (⅛in) along one long edge. Lay it diagonally across the hill and tree line layers.

Frayed edges

Lining silk (jap silk) fabrics, with torn and frayed edges, are used to represent grass lines in the midground, as shown in the detail above. This sort of silk is used as it frays more easily than others. It also has the subtle gleam that distant grass lines have.

- The Jap silk is torn and frayed to a depth of 3mm (⅛in) across the top of a horizontal layer. Two or three torn and frayed lines blend together and give the soft appearance of graded colour.

- As an alternative, you can use a slightly irregular cut line and fray each cut section separately to a depth of 3mm (⅛in). This will result in a harvested appearance.

- All frayed layers must be ironed after fraying so that the edge lies flat.

7 Layer 8 (foreground) has been torn to size and the top profile frayed by 3mm (⅛in). Once it has been laid into place, position the window to check the placements.

Shaping curves

If the design calls for it, frayed strips of the fabrics used can be shaped to fit a curved design line by using a hot iron and a fine water spray bottle. This technique requires very sharp, long-bladed embroidery scissors. It is used mainly for the cotton foregrounds that are sloped or rounded. The foreground will need an extra 2–3cm (¾–1⅛in) added to the sides and base.

In this project, the cotton foreground layer can be cut to a slightly wavering profile, or it can be torn and frayed in the same way as the silk grass layers. The foreground layer must be of a similar fabric weight as the sky; as this helps to maintain the tension of the work when lacing it over a mounting board.

1 Fray the top edge and place it flat on the ironing surface. Spray the layer evenly with water.

2 Lift and hold one side of the layer and place a hot iron onto the other side; move the iron slowly across the fabric as it is pulled in the direction of the curve needed for the design. Redo this step if necessary, then carefully re-iron and leave on the board until completely cool and dry.

3 Place the window over the layer and draw around the outside. Carefully cut off any excess from the sides.

4 Leave the foreground layer on the board until you are ready to lay it straight onto the work as it is very easy to lose the curve. Most silk layers' curves can be adjusted without spraying and ironing.

8 Prepare the branches for layer 9 as explained in 'Suede elements' below. With the window in place, place the cut branches into position.

Detail of Ultrasuede surface texture.

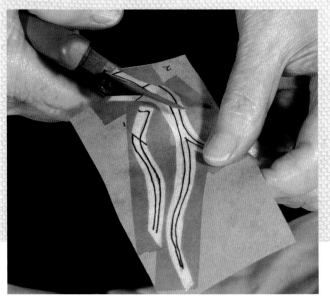

Suede elements

Ultrasuede is a man-made fabric which cuts to a sharp line, has a fine texture, does not fray and is an ideal fabric to use for elements such as tree trunks, branches and boulders.

Natural suede is expensive, but it is also reversible, as the colour is basically the same on each side. You can achieve a similar result by using fusible web to attach fine felt to coloured cotton or silk noil, in which case, the felt will end at the mounting allowance while the attached fabric extends a further 2cm (¾in).

1 Using a fine ink pen, trace the outlines of the element onto tissue paper. If necessary, make sure the lines extend into the mounting allowance.

2 Leaving an allowance of 1–2cm (⅜–¾in) on all edges, cut away the excess tissue paper. Place on the suede and tape it into place with sticky tape.

3 Cut along the traced lines. Using tweezers, place the element into position as per the design.

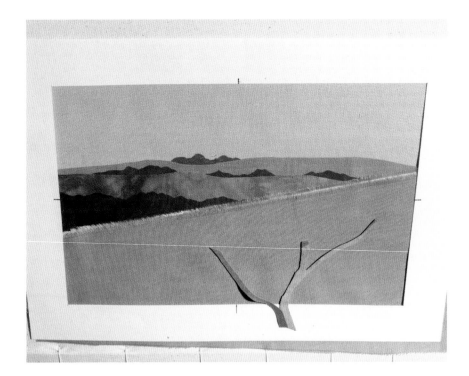

TIP

Silk organza often has tiny flaws. This doesn't usually matter, but with this work such flaws will show up. If possible, turn the piece so that any flaws are in the base of the work. Here, they will be in an area that is to be surface stitched, and will thus be better hidden.

9 Although you have been checking with the layout as you have been layering the fabrics, it is time to do a final check with the window in place and make any adjustments. It is most important that the branches for the placement of the birds' perch is accurate. The image above shows how the bird silhouettes (see page 58) are used to test the placement, as explained on page 39. The ruler and tweezers are handy for this process. Once you are satisfied, remove the silhouettes and place the white silk organza – layer 10, the overlay – over the entire background, including all mounting allowances.

The overlay

Obviously, if the overlay is not tacked (basted) into place covering the background, then the whole background will fall off!

It is important to tack the overlay in the order described below. If tacked around the whole edge in one continuous line, the layers will 'screw' slightly and the organza cannot be tensioned tightly across the fabric layers.

1 With the organza overlay tacked into position, clamp the frame to the table so that it protrudes over the table's edge. Using polycotton on a no. 9 crewel needle, begin by tacking along the top edge of the sky.

2 If necessary, turn and re-clamp the frame to the table; then tack the lower edge, tensioning the organza layer only against the top line of tacking.

3 Tack one side making sure all layers are stitched down. Then tack the second side and again tension it against the first.

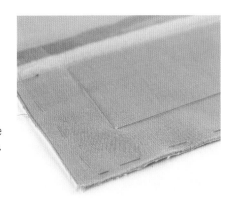

This detail shows the tacking line at the bottom left corner. The lines of blue tacking are separate, not continuous.

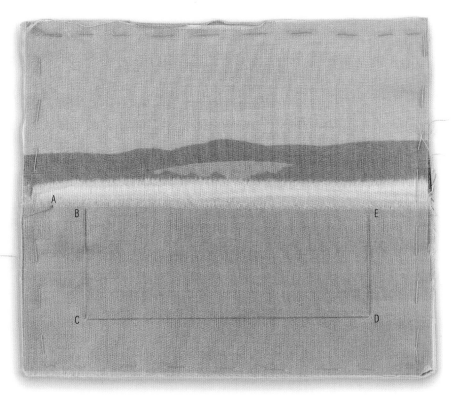

The isolation stitches

The isolation stitches are three long stitches (shown in orange above) that will isolate the area to be stitched from the mounting allowances. If heavily stitched, the mounting allowance will not fold smoothly under a board when it is laced ready for framing.

1 Place the window into position over the background. Tie a knot at the end of the thread and take the needle down through the mounting allowance (A), bringing it up on the inside of the window approximately halfway along the left-hand side (B). Take the first long stitch to the left base-line corner (C).

2 After taking a tiny stitch, bring the needle up and take the second long stitch to the right side base corner (D). Take another tiny stitch, then bring the needle up and take the third long stitch to around the halfway point inside the right side of the window (E).

3 Remove the window and bring the needle up into the mounting allowance and finish off with a couple of small stitches. Pull the thread through to the surface and clip off.

BACK STITCHING

Due to the design here, the manner of stitching the layers in this project is slightly different from the standard approach described on page 53. Here, the foremost tree line (1) only covers the left half of the background, and there is no other line that runs from mounting allowance to mounting allowance. Therefore the hill line (4) with its design lines must be stitched as described in the work plan below.

For the best results, use the same colour throughout; do not try to match the thread to a specific layer. I use DMC 3022 for most back stitching worked on a blue or green background, 3776 for terracotta desert backgrounds and 746 for cream to white in seascapes and snow. As always, there are exceptions to the rule.

You will need

- No. 9 crewel needle
- Stranded cotton: DMC 3022

Land lines

Back stitching order of work

4
2
3(i)   3(ii)   3(iii)
1
5

1 – Tree line
2 – Hill line
3(i), (ii) and (iii) – Tree lines
4 – Hill line
5 – Perches

Back stitch work plan

Using a no. 9 crewel needle and a single strand of DMC 3022 stranded cotton throughout, work your back stitch according to the surface stitchery diagram opposite. Remember to stitch the indentations of the tree line of the first layer, and any design lines drawn in others.

1   Back stitch the tree line marked 1, working from right to left edge. Stitch indentations (see below) where needed.

2   Back stitch the hill line marked 2 from the grasslines, working from the right to the left edge.

3   Working as above, back stitch the three sections of the tree line; marked 3(i), (ii) and (iii).

4   Back stitch the hill line marked 4, working from the centre outwards. Stitch the hill line details marked with dotted lines. Complete the other side, but leave the rearmost tree line unstitched (see right).

5   Check the placement of the perches (5) in the foreground before placing the birds. This is described in more detail on page 68.

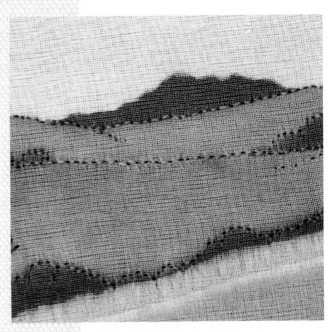

Enlarged detail of the back stitch on the embroidery. Note that the rearmost tree line is not stitched.

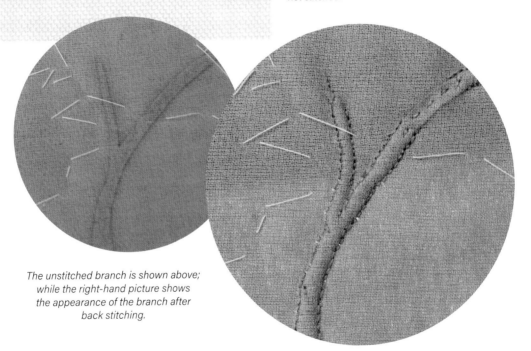

The unstitched branch is shown above; while the right-hand picture shows the appearance of the branch after back stitching.

Indentations

Indentations are the small curving shapes cut to form the canopy of tree lines. They are shown as small stitches taken from the back stitched line into the tree line fabric. They give detail and lock the line into position. Without them, the fabric will pull away when foreground surface stitching – such as grass – is worked.

Back stitching the perches

It is important that the branches upon which the finches are perched are accurately placed before they are back stitched.

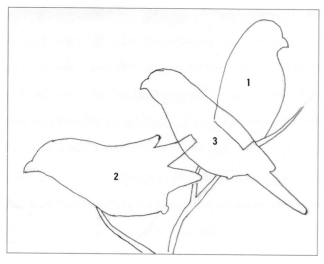

1 From the master copy (see page 59), take an accurate copy, on tissue paper, of the birds on their perches. Trace out the individual birds and cut a silhouette of each on black card (alternatively, you can use the existing silhouettes you made – see page 68). These can be taped together if needed. Hold the bird tracing in position over the branches and check the placement. If needed, carefully adjust the branches, using the point of a needle through the organza, to move them into place.

2 Once in place, tack the outline of the birds into position over the branches. Remove the tissue by running the head of a needle along the tacked line and gently pull the tissue away. Check the branches' placement against the master copy.

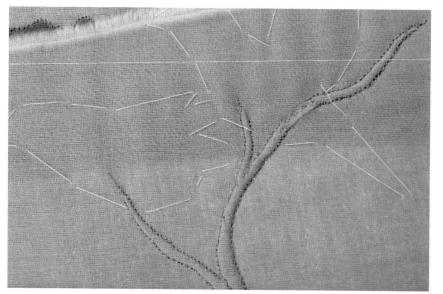

3 Begin back stitching the perches at the top of the left-hand perch. Back stitch 1–1.5cm (½–⅝in) along one side of the branch, then take the needle down to the back and bring it up on the opposite side of the branch. Stitch for the same distance before repeating the process and swapping sides again. Continue alternating the stitched intervals until you reach the base line, stitch into the mounting allowance for 1mm (⅟₁₆in) and then work your way back to the start, filling in the gaps. Stitch the other branch in the same manner.

4 This completes the back stitching. Keep hold of the taped-together silhouettes, as they can be used as a guide for the next section, when working the surface stitching of the foreground grasses.

PROJECT ONE

TIP

Should the shape begin to bounce away from the stitch line as you work the back stitch, push it gently back into place with the point of the needle and continue to 'tamp' it into place with a small stitch.

SURFACE STITCHING

This is the most exciting part of the project, the surface stitchery on-frame, followed by the application of all stitched elements made off-frame.

As the background fabrics are layered, so is the surface stitchery, which gives further depth and dimension to the work. To gain the low-relief inherent in my work, work in the following way:

- from the middle ground to the foreground;
- from the centre of the work out to the sides;
- from the surface of the background up into relief.

Adding the surface stitchery and stitched elements over the overlay is the part of the process that I find most creative and enjoyable. Do take your time as you develop and add further depth to the work with this stage.

Threads for the birds.

You will need

Number of strands of DMC stranded cotton – all single strand unless shown (2).

MIDDLE GROUND THREADS
- Tree structures – 3787
- Dead trees – 3024
- Shrubbery and canopies – 3346/3347 (2 – one of each)

GRASSES
- Layer 1 and grass heads – 746
- Layer 2 and grass heads – 746 + 3047 (intermixed)
- Layer 3 – 3047 + 3053 (intermixed)
- Layer 4 – 3053 + 3052 (intermixed)

FLORA
- Structure – 3052
- Leaves – 3053/52 (2 – one of each)
- Flowers – Blanc (2)
- Centres – 680 (2)

BIRDS
- Eye and rump flashes – 666
- Top of head, neck and throat – 3023
- Back shading to wings – 3348 > 581 > 580
- Belly – 3024 > 3023
- Tail – 3787
- Legs – 3064

Threads for the midground, grasses and flora.

Making changes

Now is the time to make any changes, as it is not possible once stitching has started. This is because replacing stitches will tear the organza overlay. You might need to make changes to accommodate any movement of the fabric layers during cutting, layering and back stitching, or you may wish to extend the grasses or another foreground shrub or flora. If changes are necessary, write or sketch in any changes to the placement of the trees and shrubs on layout copy 2, as shown here. In particular, note the following:

Midground

- When working the trees, stitch the structures first, then the canopies.

Foreground

- Start by stitching the branchlets.
- Next, work the four grass layers. The 'dot-dash' line highlighted in blue marks the approximate top edge of the grass layer.
- Next, work the shrubbery lines. The 'three dots-dash' lines highlighted in orange marks the approximate top edge of the foreground shrubbery.
- Next, add the birds, working from the most distant (1) to the nearest (3).

Planning the work in this way helps to prevent the stitched area from being excessively rubbed by hand or thread and helps smooth out any puckering or distortion.

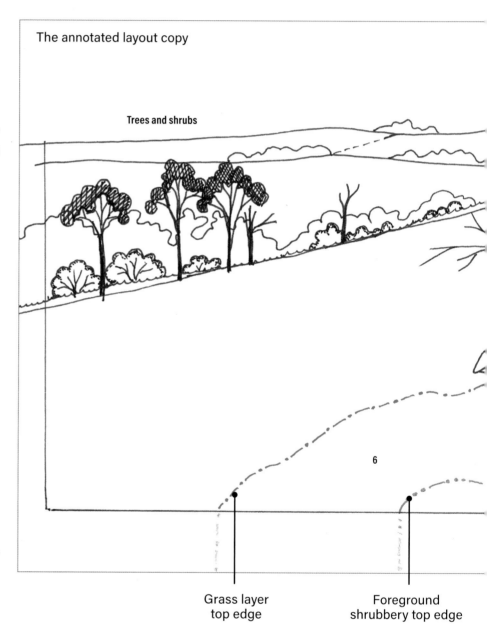

The annotated layout copy

Trees and shrubs

6

Grass layer top edge

Foreground shrubbery top edge

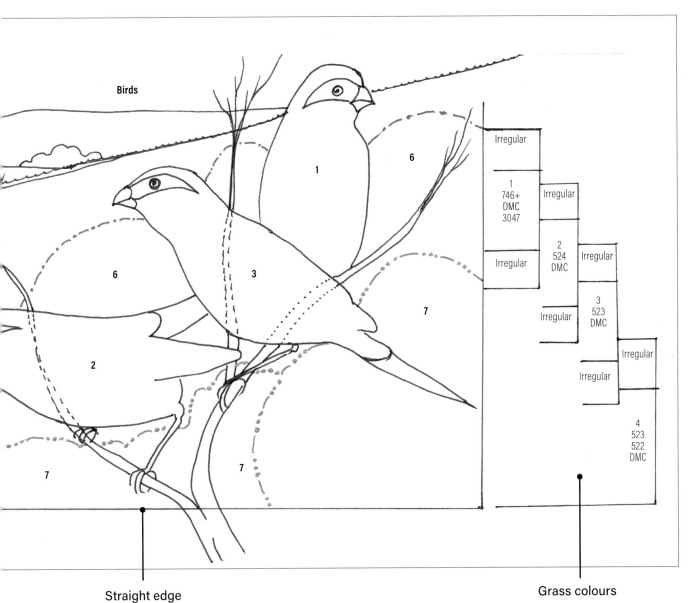

Birds

Irregular

1
746+
DMC
3047

Irregular

2
524
DMC

Irregular

3
523
DMC

Irregular

Irregular

Irregular

Irregular

4
523
522
DMC

Straight edge

*This is the base line of the work and heavy stitching
does not go into the mounting allowances.*

Grass colours

*This side panel shows how to work the four
grass layers. This is explained in more detail
on page 83.*

On-frame surface stitching

To help break down the general techniques for surface stitching, the sampler on pages 78–79 shows how the structures of common stitched elements, such as trees and shrubs, are built up, along with the stitching processes. The specifics for this project are included alongside each element.

Before you begin, it is a good idea to check the tension of the frame, and, if necessary, adjust it. The tension at this point should be slightly tighter due to the back stitching. All the surface stitching, particularly the grass layers, will become a part of a heavily-stitched mid- and foreground.

If for any reason it has slackened, it must be re-tensioned by over stitching one long side before further work can proceed. To do so, do not remove the original lacing: simply stitch over it by taking a further 'bite' of approximately 10mm (½in) into the calico layer only, adjacent to the previous stitch and pull the fabric tightly towards the frame. Never stitch through any of the work fabric layers (including the organza overlay) or the work will be distorted.

Work plan for surface stitching

Keep both the master copy and your annotated layout copy 2 (see pages 74–75) to hand for reference as you work.

On-frame

1 Check the placement of the birds and their alignment with the perches.

2 Check the midground area, change as needed, then completely stitch the trees and shrubs.

3 Stitch the grass layers one at a time from the top to the baseline.

4 Stitch all of the structures of the shrubbery.

5 Complete all of the flora: petals, leaves and centres.

Off-frame

6 Stitch the birds and any other elements and prepare them for:

On-frame

7 Cut and stitch the beak onto the bird.

8 Stitch the bird into place.

9 Stitch the eyes and the legs into place.

10 Fill in any gaps around the body of the bird.

In this project, the trees and shrubbery in the middle distance also give the appearance of interspersed woodland areas glimpsed between the hills. The order in which you approach things is critical.

Adapted feather stitch

This stitch is my essential way of stitching all trees and shrubbery, as well as some other flora – and the only real difference between these is that, when used for a tree, the stitch is worked with a longer catch stitch that, when wrapped, becomes the trunk of the tree. The shorter flower structures can be either utilized to be elongated or to become a mound.

In this project, the stitch is used for both trees and varying flower structures, so it is worth practising. The catch stitch can align with other such groups or form a long stitch for a part of the trunk of a tree. Other than this, exactly the same stitching sequence is adapted. The sampler explores these different ways of using it.

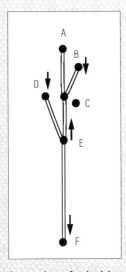

The order of stitching

Up at A; down at B; up at C in the loop and pull through. The thread is taken across and down at D and brought up in the loop, in line at E and down at F.

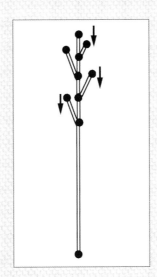

This example shows how the same sequence of stitches can be made in an extended form, giving an upright structure more suited to a tall tree.

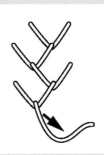

TIP

The main difference between the traditional stitch and my adapted version is that the thread is held in a straight line and the stitches alternate (left or right) on either side of the central held line, which is realigned after each stitch.

The result is a straight central line rather than the zigzag result of traditional feather stitch, shown here.

The stitch sampler

Here I have collected together all the key stitches used in one place. You may wish to make your own version before you start, so that you can practise and gather stitches together for easy reference. Use this sampler in combination with the work plan and the annotated layout copy on pages 74–75. It is divided into the following four parts, each of which is tackled in turn over the following pages.

Trees – pages 80–81

Every country has its own specific trees and Australia is no different. The melaleuca, the banksia, the acacia and the eucalyptus are just a few. In fact, many countries have adopted the eucalyptus and acacia (wattle) as their own, just as Australians have adopted many of the pines and deciduous trees of the northern hemisphere.

The trees I have chosen for the sampler and projects is the eucalyptus, though the same structure will suit many other forms found in the open habitats used in this project. I have used the same adapted feather stitch for all trees and canopies in the middle ground.

Grasses – pages 82–85

Grasses are found throughout the land – from hardy windswept grasses of coastlines and deserts; to the softer and more delicate grasses of meadows, fields and plains; to those clinging to the rocky platforms of ranges and mountains. There are many varieties of grass. They are all plants with long narrow leaves, a hollow jointed stem with flower spikes or inflorescences of clusters of membranous flowers. Without the grass family, our world would be a very different place.

Take the time to observe the structure of grass in a field. You will find that the bulk of the grass is in the leaf and stem, that the colour is deeper at the base, blending subtly and paling as it recedes into the distance. You may also notice that the base of the grass plant often has a different colour within its structure; these colours can be fine terracotta or mauve streaks along the stem and, stitched in small amounts, add definition to the base of the grass layers.

Most grasses species flower or seed at the same time. You will note that to the right of the grass layers there are three different structures of grass flower spikes.

Shrubbery – pages 86–87

Flowering shrubs are many and varied, being found in almost all habitats that birds frequent. From the low windswept and tip-pruned species of the coastlines, to the understoreys of the rain forests into wooded areas of the tablelands and plains. In Australia, where I live, some are colourful; such as the many grevillea species which the honeyeaters and spinebills love to sip from. Some, such as Sturt's desert rose (*Gossypium sturtianum*), have large exuberant flowers; while others have small, clustered flowers: the native daphne (*Eriostemon myoporoides*), called the fairy wax flower in some regions, is a good example of this. The fringe myrtle (*Calytrix tetragona*) produces small nut-like fruit. All attract insects, which in turn attract insect-eaters like robins and wrens.

The shrub used here is the snowy daisy-bush (*Olearia lirata*). A bushy upright shrub that grows to 5m (16½ft), it has sticky oblong alternating leaves with white daisy-like flower heads. I am sure you could find a shrub you could exchange for the one I am depicting here.

Flowers – pages 88–89

There are as many differing flower shapes as there are differing ways of depicting them with the simple stitches mentioned, always remember that the structure of flowers are an indication only of shape and colour: they are not meant to be a botanical drawing. On the sampler there are several examples of flowers that could be used on other projects and, of course, there are many others for you to find in your own regions.

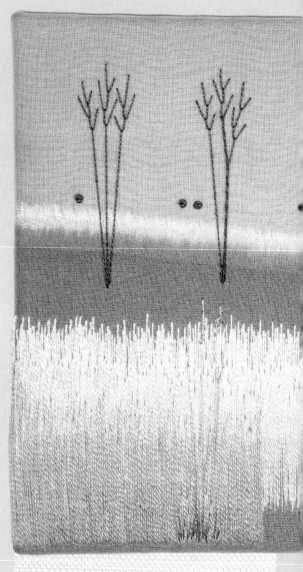

Understanding the sampler

The number of green French knots on the sampler shows to which stage the various examples have been built up. Small straight stitches refer to different layers of grass or types of flowers.

Stitch movements and thread directions are indicated as follows:

- Upward red arrow = thread up.
- Downwards red arrow = thread down.
- Red thread shows the placement of grass layers.
- Red thread is used to show the wrapping sequences (labelled I, II and III).
- Red thread is stitched to show the fly stitch where it connects one group of stitches to another and extends a structure's height.

Trees

The first four stages show the process of embroidering a simple tree. It can also be used as the central trunk of the next three complex tree shapes.

Grasses

This areas shows the three layers of grasses and flower spikes.

Shrubbery

These build up from basic to complex in seven stages.

Flowers

Techniques for various shapes of flower heads and leaves.

Trees

The structures of all trees within a grouping are stitched first, followed by the canopies. The stitch used for the structure is an adapted feather stitch described on page 77.

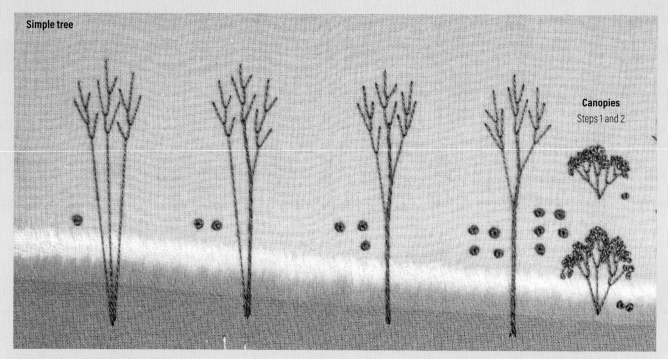

Simple tree

Canopies
Steps 1 and 2

Simple tree (stages 1–4)

- Estimate the height of the tree. Thread a no. 9 crewel needle with a single strand of deep grey-brown DMC 3787 stranded cotton (use pale-greenish grey DMC 3024 for dead trees). Bring the needle up from the back at the tallest point of the tree. Pull the thread through and lay it in a straight line to the proposed base of the tree – usually in the frayed areas of the grass line and foreground. Take three small feather stitches on alternating sides of the thread. Between each stitch, realign the thread in a straight line to the base of the tree. This gives a straight line between each stitch, not the zigzag line of the traditional feather stitch. The angle of the stitch should be acute. Complete the first group of feather stitches with a long catch stitch to the base of the tree. Repeat on either side of the first group, beginning a little lower each time. On each group of three modified feather stitches, make a long catch stitch ending at the same point – the base of the tree.

- Bring the thread up at the bottom 'V' or junction of the first group of feather stitches and, from the right, make three to four wraps around the central catch stitch. It is important to always wrap from the right to the left. Take the thread to the right and wrap the right group's catch stitch in the same way, drawing it towards the central trunk and continue wrapping to the base of the tree. The wrapping should be tight enough to pull the catch stitches into the trunk. When you have finished each wrapping, give the thread a gentle tug to align the wraps and anchor the thread slightly to one side of the central trunk to give it a base.

- We now need to wrap the left catch stitch into the trunk. Work as before, making two to three wraps after the joining of the right group to the trunk. Sweep the needle from the right side under all the catch stitches, drawing in the left group to the main trunk and wrap to the base. Anchor the thread at the base of the tree to complete the simple tree structure.

Adding a canopy (stage 5)

The example canopies shown are worked in two steps, using two strands of DMC 3347, 3346, (greens) – one of each on a no. 9 needle.

- Make a rounded canopy of French knots using two wraps across the tops of the feather-stitched groups, forming a series of curved interlocking lines that cross or link into each other.

- Return and fill in under the canopies with one or two wrap knots and with one at each end of the canopy's curves, tapering them to give a lacy irregular effect. Always complete one tree at a time and leave the occasional bare branch.

Should you want to show the tree in flower or with new growth, use one strand of the flower colour alone with one strand of the lightest green used along the top curves of the canopies. This allows the colours to blend into the body, avoiding the heaviness of a single colour. Observe the trees around you for colour ideas.

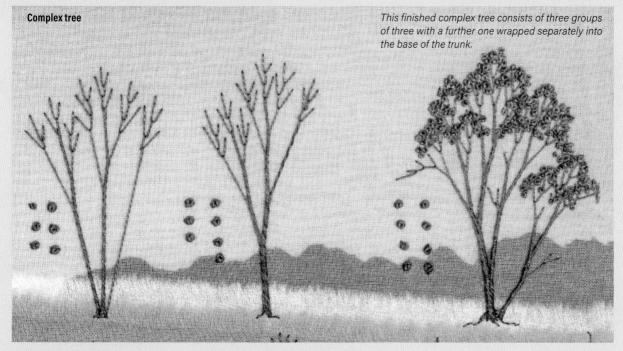

Complex tree

This finished complex tree consists of three groups of three with a further one wrapped separately into the base of the trunk.

Developing your trees further (stages 6–8)

Further complexity can be added to the simple trees using straight, fly or slanted buttonhole stitches to alter or extend a canopy, or to add interest to the branches. Take care to slot any changes realistically into the branch to be extended. Remember that the angle of the stitch will need to be acute, not a right angle.

A junction is best attained by gently pulling the branch to one side and inserting the needle into the background (not the branch), then bringing the needle up at the next point required for further work; or by wrapping the stitch into the branch and down to the base of the trunk finishing off with a tiny back stitch.

The line of the trunk can also be altered by using the tips of two needles. One is used to gently pull the trunk into a position and pushing it through into the background to hold it in place; the other is placed above or below to ensure there are no sharp angles, and to adjust the line of the trunk. Bring a threaded needle up at the point of the top needle and couch the trunk into place, ensuring the stitches lie between the wrapped threads, then take it down at the next needle point. To finish, carefully pull the couched stitches and trunk into place and make a small back stitch at its base.

Obviously, the height of a complex tree will be greater than the earlier examples, so it would be a good idea to trial a few trees on a separate rigid frame rather than your actual work.

- Start by creating a simple tree, following the instructions opposite. Always begin with an initial group of three, to which can be added a single group of one, two or three on either side. Wrap each separately.

- Next, we need to wrap the groups to the central trunk. Begin by bringing the thread up in the right-hand group. Wrap the right-hand group into the central group, followed by the left side down to the base, forming the trunk. Take the thread down a little to one side of the base.

Grasses

It is the open grassy fields or meadows, bordered by woodland shrubbery, that we will use for the first layers of the surface stitchery on the foreground. To me, the grass layers of this form of landscape are the most important, as they allow colour, depth and give a sense of distance to the work.

The shape of the grass itself suggests that the stitch to be used needs to be a long straight stitch. I use an adaptation of a laid stitch (see page 158). This is used rather than a satin stitch as it prevents a bulky build-up of thread at the back of the work, giving a smoother surface.

Once completed, grass can become the basis of a work in its own right or it can be partially obscured by further stitchery of the flora.

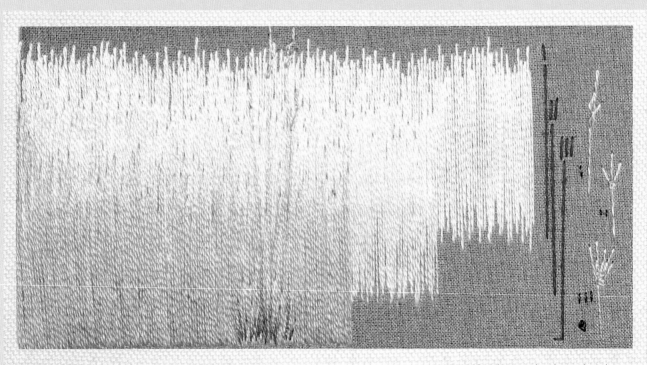

Laid stitch

Laid stitch is a traditional crewel embroidery filling stitch where the edges conform to a specific shape. I have adapted this stitch so that the top and bottom of each stitch are completely irregular within the space to be stitched on the foreground, except for the bottom layer of the stitches which form a straight line along the base of the work. This irregularity enhances the tonal blending of a grass layer.

Note that the sampler shows three layers; there are four used in the project.

Planning the grass layers

You can design a work where the grass layers are stitched across the whole foreground with an irregular but relatively straight line encroaching on the frayed grass layers of the background, or you can have an off-centre dip indicating a change in the lie of the land – again, stitched across the foreground as described.

In this project, the grass layers are designed to emphasize the diagonal line of the foreground, in order to give further tension and movement to the work. On the second layout or tracing copy of the master design (see pages 74–75) a dotted and dashed line indicates the curving line of the top of the first grass layer. On the right-hand side I have drawn a diagram of the four individual grass layers (a detail of this is shown to the right). There is a 'box' area on the top and bottom of each layer indicating the irregular area of the stitching. Layer 4 is the exception. Here, the base line is straight, indicating that all these stitches will be in a straight line at the base of the work. In each layer I have noted the colour of the threads to be used.

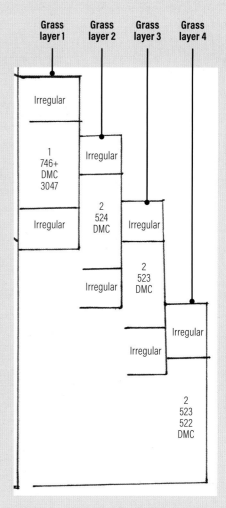

Detail of the grass area box from the layout design, highlighting the colours used for each part of each layer.

The colour of grass

The colour of grass changes according to the seasons. The dull colours of winter blend into the new creamy-green growth of spring; into the rich green golds of summer; and in turn into the golden yellows and terracottas of autumn; then, completing the cycle, back to the dull brown yellows of winter.

Below are my suggestions of colours that could be used for the grass layers. The main criterion is that they blend from the palest to the deepest colour at the baseline of the work.

- Spring into summer – greens: DMC 524, 523, 522 or 746, 3053 and 3052
- Summer into autumn – pale yellows into golds: DMC 746, 3053, 3047, 3046
- Autumn into winter – golds into browns: 3047, 3033, 3032
- Base colours (small amounts for emphasis): mauve, terracotta, grey-green, brown: 3042, 3776, 3022, 3790.

Stitching the grass layers

Use one strand on a no. 9 needle throughout. With the frame clamped to a table, tack in the top line of the grass area. Have to hand both the master design and the second copy showing the surface stitching plan for reference.

1 Thread the needle with one strand of the palest colour (DMC 746) and knot the tail of the thread before clipping off the end. The first stitches in this layer are guide stitches. Bring the needle up at the middle of the tacked line, and make stitches measuring approximately 3–3.5cm (1⅛–1⅜in) deep and 1–2cm (⅜–¾in) apart towards the right isolating stitch. Do not stitch within the outline of the birds at this point.

2 Next, use tiny, irregularly placed straight stitches between each stitch. These stitches tamp down any bulging or puckering that might otherwise occur and prevent any further movement between the fabric layers. Return to the centre and repeat the guide stitches to where the stitched layer ends. Again, stitch back to the centre point using tiny stitches.

3 Beginning at the right side, fill in the first layer. Apart from the early upright stitches on the right side, angle the remaining stitches to approximately 20 degrees. Maintain the angle of the stitch as well as the irregularity at the top and bottom of the stitch, making sure that it is particularly irregular along the top edge. The stitching should completely cover the fabric. This completes layer 1. From this point all layers should be stitched to cover the outlines but not the whole of the birds – check the placement of the birds periodically, as shown below.

4 Stitch layer 2 from the right, maintaining the same angles and using DMC 3053 shaded with DMC 746. Make sure that it blends irregularly into the top layer.

5 Layer 3 is stitched as above, using DMC 3052 shaded with 3053. The left side of this layer requires only a few stitches of this colour, due to the angle of the stitches and the slope of the foreground. Make sure that some parts of the layer will be straight along the base line of the work.

This detail shows grass layer 1 complete and grass layer 2 begun.

Use the cardboard silhouettes you made earlier to re-check the placement of the birds over the grass layers as you work, as noted in step 3.

6. Make the final layer (layer 4) using DMC 3052, and with the same blending irregularity at the top of the stitching. The base line should be made completely straight along the inner edge of the mounting allowance.

7. Check the completed layers. If you feel you need further stitches to help with the blending between colours, add them by slotting them between stitches. Always finish off with a tiny back stitch at the bottom of the stitch or between stitches.

Grass layers complete.

Grass flower spikes

The flower spikes add detail to the grass layers and are superimposed across the layers. They may fall above the top of the first layer, in the frayed background area, or be scattered throughout the body of the grass. For this work I have placed them mainly above or into the first layer because much of the area under the birds will be over-stitched with shrubbery.

There are many grass varieties, each with their own particular flower spike. The spike used in this project is based on the native grasses found in the fields near where I live. However, it could be used to describe any similar grass species with long slender delicate flower spikes.

The grass flowers and stems are a mix of greens (DMC 3053) and creams (DMC 746) using a single strand of stranded cotton.

The stitch used is an adapted twisted chain stitch with variations; the last stitch having a long catch stitch, forming the stem, which is inserted into the body of the grass area.

Three different varieties of grass spikes.

Adapted twisted chain stitch

Unlike the close traditional twisted chain stitch, which tends to form a cord-like appearance, these stitches are elongated and open. As a variation, the first twisted chain stitch can be repeated. If you are left-handed, reverse the stitch sequence. You can find a diagram and more information on page 159, in the stitch glossary.

1. The top section of the stitch needs to be made the same length as the 'loop' of the stitch. To achieve this, bring the needle up at the top of the spike; the thread is held in the direction the grass stem is to be stitched.

2. Take the needle down 0.5cm (¼in) to the left of the thread and bring it up in line with the previous stitch, within the loop that forms naturally.

3. Pull the thread through to form the first twisted chain. Do not make a catch stitch.

4. On the right side, bring the needle down and away 1–2mm (⅟₁₆in) from the middle of the loop. Holding the thread in the left hand, flip it over as you pull it through to form a 'cross' above the held loop. Bring the needle up into the loop and in line with the first stitch and pull through. Each of the two stitches should be approximately 0.5cm (¼in) long.

5. End with a long catch stitch into the body of the grass or the base of the work, maintaining the angle of the stitches forming a stem.

Shrubbery

The structures of all shrubs or flora are stitched across the designed area before any flowers are added. The main reason for this is that all shrubs and most herbaceous flora will have the same basic structure. Working in this manner also helps to maintain a relationship with each layer and placement, particularly if stitching differing flowers across the foreground.

　　The only difference between the structure of the shrubbery and the trees is in the length of the catch stitch which forms the tree's trunk.

Shrubbery in progress over the completed grass.

Stitching the stems

The stem structures are made with the same adapted feather stitch (see page 77) used for the trees, and using a single strand of stranded cotton in a deep green such as DMC 3051 on a no. 9 crewel needle. The central stem of the adapted feather stitch is always vertical, unless the stem is aimed in a diagonal direction. The stitch sequence consists of a group of three similar elements. Remember to make the angles of the stitches acute.

1　Begin at the uppermost point of the stem. Bring the thread through into position and hold it down in a straight line towards the base of the stem. Take the needle across 3–5mm (⅛–¼in) to the right, below the top of the first stitch. Take the needle down.

2　Bring the needle up in the loop in line with the held thread and pull through. Take the needle 3–5mm (⅛–¼in) across to the left below the top of the second stitch. Take the needle down, bringing it up in the loop in line with the central stitches and pull through.

3　Make the catch stitch by taking the needle down approximately one stitch length in line. This extends the first sequence. Next, bring the needle up to the right in position for the next sequence.

The shrubbery, partway through working. The flowers of snowy daisy bush have brown-yellow centres, arranged in clusters at the end of branchlets. It thrives on the edges of open woodlands around watercourses.

Stems with feather stitch and fly stitch

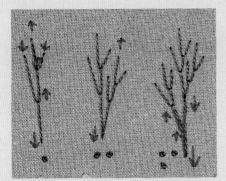

Detail of the sampler.

Use the detail to the left as a guide to the feather stitch sequences. As usual, the red arrows indicate stitch movements.

- The example on the left shows the initial structure created by following the steps above. It is identical to that of the trees earlier (see pages 80–81), except that the catch stitch is shorter.
- In the central example, the thread is now angled in a straight line to the base of the catch stitch and the above sequence is completed with its catch stitch taken into the base of the first.
- For the right-hand example, the needle is brought up on the left side above the base of the joined catch stitches. The thread is now angled to a point approximately one stitch length below the central line. The final stitch sequence is now made and joined to the others with a fly stitch by bringing the needle down at the base of the first two catch stitches, up in the loop at the above-mentioned point on the central line and down one stitch length forming the catch stitch. As shown, the fly stitch, worked in red, connects and extends the height of the stem.

Variations

There are at least two ways to extend the shape and height of this structure using the same basic sequence – the rounded structure for naturally rounded shrubs, and the elongated structural form, found in herbaceous flora.

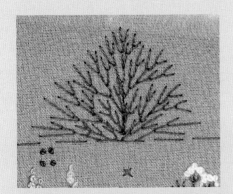

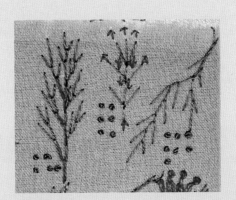

Rounded shrubs Making a structure suitable for a mound-shaped flowering shrub is nearly identical to the process for the examples opposite. The difference is that that the sequence is repeated on either side, then joined with a fly stitch. This results in a shorter spreading structure. These appear in the project under the trees in the midground.

The topmost stitches must maintain a curve and the base of the mound align with the base of the work. Working alternate sides of the mound will help maintain the curve. I make a light pencil mark approximately 2cm (¾in) into the mounting allowance, shown as a red cross, and after the upper stitch sequences, I aim the thread and stitch towards this mark. Stitching towards this mark allows the mid- and baseline branchlets to fall short of the central stem of the shrub, making it appear more natural.

At times, stitches will need to cross over each other – allow it to happen. At other times, gaps will appear: ignore them until the whole shrub is stitched, then return and angle straight, fly or small groups of two to three feather stitches into the gaps, maintaining the lines and angles of the structure. If you extend the length of the connecting fly stitches in the mound structure, the shrub will be taller and narrower. The red thread on the left side shows added groups of stitches to fill the mound. As usual, enjoy experimenting.

Structural form In the example above left, the first three groups of stitches are made in the same way as the examples opposite. The thread is then brought up on the right side to stitch groups alternating from right to left for as many times as needed.

You will note that the right side connects to the base of the previous catch stitch at the central line, and the left side connects and extends with a fly stitch, as shown in red. Occasionally you may find that you need more or fewer stitches in a sequence; in such cases it is important to maintain the alternating sequence above by putting in or leaving out the stitch concerned.

The example above centre shows traditional fern stitch, which is a member of the straight stitch family. This is normally worked from the top to the base. It is also the only way to form opposing stitch placement against the alternating leaf or flower positions on a plant.

The example above right is adapted feather stitch worked as a trailing form suited to creepers and vines. It can be worked in all directions.

Flowers

The flowers (see the lower right-hand side of the sampler on pages 78–79) may be stitched at the tops and junctions of the stems using applicable colours and simple stitches such as French and Italian knots, detached chain with varied-size catch stitches, fly and straight stitches. The leaves are stitched last using detached chains or straight stitches angled into the stems and are placed more to the base of the work.

For the flower used in the project, the snowy daisy bush, I am using French knots for both the buds and petals combined with straight or detached chain stitches for the leaves.

Complete all of the flowers and buds before placing the leaves. Using one or two strands of stranded cotton (DMC 3042 or a suitable green) on a no. 9 needle, place straight stitches as needed towards the top of the structures. Towards the base, use detached chain stitches so that the catch stitch is angled to the stems.

French knots

Stitching French knots on a rigid frame is very satisfying as you are in complete control of the exact placement of the knot. This is because the stitch is a stab stitch not a slipped stitch.

Thread a no. 7 crewel needle with two strands of stranded cotton: DMC Blanc for the buds and petals and DMC 680 for the centre. Bring the needle through at the exact place required, wrap the thread around the point of the needle once and reinsert it a thread's distance away. Pull the thread tightly around the needle and, holding it firmly, gently pull the needle through allowing the thread to slide down the needle and the wrapped knot to rest on the surface of the work. Firmly pull the thread through to the back ready for the next knot.

For larger knots, use more strands and larger needles, not more wraps. The buds are arranged on the tops of the structures in a slightly rounded manner and the flowers are a small cup of three French knots with a single knot within the cup on the tops and the junctions of the structures, as shown on the sampler.

Daisy
Five variations of stitches can be used for daisy-type flowers, using respectively: French knots; double French knots; double cross stitch; and detached chain with differing catch stitches.

Flower with five petals
This was made using tightly pulled detached chain stitch with a long catch stitch. This approach is suited to many common varieties of flower.

Four variations
This shows how different groupings and placements of French knots can be used to easily alter the shapes of the flowers.

Lace flower

This is an example of how the structure allows the flower's shape. It is stitched in the same manner as the feather stitch structure, except that the last stitch of the group forms a 'claw' and the catch stitches all come together to form a central claw. The flowers then form a canopy across the claw. Other canopy-style flora are fennel, pin cushions, spiraea and agapanthus.

Hardenbergia

This is also good for other pea-shaped flora. It uses two slanted detached chain stitches at the top of the flower and a fly stitch at the base. Each has very small catch stitches meeting together. A small, one-wrap French knot is placed at the junction.

Spider flower

Use detached chain stitches with an Italian knot stitch as a catch stitch for this form of grevillea.

Clematis

This is made up of a circle of straight stitches in combination with Italian knot stitch, with one large French knot at the centre.

Mulla mulla

Use stacked fly stitches with a straight stitch to taper the top of this compact perennial. It has a trailing feather stitch as a structure, with chains as leaves.

Off-frame stitchery

The only surface elements to be worked off-frame for this project are the birds. Each is hand-stitched individually on a hoop. The body of each bird is stitched on firm, unwashed calico, on an embroidery hoop using a closely-packed elongated stem stitch (see page 156). The bill, eyes, legs and claws are stitched or applied separately.

You will need

- Embroidery hoop of a suitable size
- Sharp scissors (fabric and embroidery), tweezers, forceps, stuffing tool
- Needles – nos. 9, 7
- Fine black pen
- Good quality calico, Vliesofix, threads – stranded cottons

Preparation

On a piece of layout paper make a separate tracing of each bird. Where one underlaps another, draw an allowance of 1–2cm (½–¾in) away from the area and draw a dotted line at the point where they meet. Include all linear details such as wing, bill and eye positions, and draw in any distinct colour changes that are indicative of the species – but keep it simple, as in the examples here. Number each bird according to the order of placement on the work.

The planned stitch direction and DMC thread colours are noted here.

Transferring the line drawings to the calico

A separate piece of calico is needed for each bird. The calico and the hoop used must be large enough to accommodate the full size of the bird. Transfer each line drawing onto its calico piece using a fine black ink pen. Do not use pencil, because the graphite will be pulled through by the thread with each stitch. Use a backlit window if a light box isn't handy, and ensure the bird is centred on the hoop.

Make sure the wing position, the actual size of the eye ring and where the beak meets the head are drawn accurately – you will never stitch the beak or the eye.

On the body, indicate with black ink arrows the flow of the feathers giving the direction to be taken by the stitches. Draw a largish arrow pointing away from the back of the bird. The thread will always fall towards this arrow.

Transferred design on calico

This red-browed grass finch design was not used in the final project, but serves as an example of how to plan the stitch direction on the calico.

Fabric calico

Good-quality calico is often quite hard to obtain. It is easy to pick the poorer quality; the weave is quite open, but it appears firm due to the amount of dressing in the fabric, if this is the only calico you can find, shrink it. There are two ways to do this:

The first is to boil it in a pot. Completely cover the calico with water, bring to the boil and boil for five minutes. Allow it to cool in the pot to allow all dressing to be reabsorbed.

The second approach is to pour enough boiling water to completely cover the calico, then wait until it cools completely. Once dry, shrink the fabric again using a hot iron on the high steam setting. It is a good idea to use an ironing cloth as the dressing scorches easily.

Stitching the bird

The stitch used initially is a slightly elongated stem stitch (see page 155). As the work progresses, this is further elongated to 8–10mm (¼–³⁄₈in). I much prefer using this stitch to the traditional long and short stitch, as it gives better coverage of the base fabric which is needed when the bird is stuffed as it is applied to the work

1 Place the calico in the hoop and tension tightly. Depending on the type of feather, use one or two strands of stranded cotton on a no. 7 crewel needle (I have used a single strand because the feathers of this finch are fine and silky, but you can use two). Begin stitching by weaving the thread through the body of the bird, coming up from the back of the work at the point where the bill meets the head at the top of the bird.

2 Using a slightly elongated stem stitch just outside the outline, work from the head along the back to where the tail joins the body, allowing the thread to fall towards the arrow.

3 Turn the hoop and commence stitching back towards the head. The 'under' stitches taken should be very small. They are taken by pushing the surface of the stitch of the previous row aside with the point of the needle; a small stitch is taken either side of those taken previously. This 'double' stitching is worked throughout, giving depth to the feathers.

4 Continue stitching, turning and stacking the surface lines as closely as possible in the above manner, following the colour changes and maintaining the stitch direction of the feathers by back filling spaces as needed. As the work progresses – usually by the third row – further elongate the stitch to 8–10mm (¼–³⁄₈in). Adjust the stitch length according to the curvature of the body.

Notes on stitching birds

- Always work from the head and the back of the bird downwards to the belly. Stitch the head, the back and the rump, then fill in the area of the neck and complete the wings. Fill in from the base of the bill into the throat, the breast and the belly so that the last line of stitching will be slightly smaller and just over the bird's outline.

- Where there is a colour change (see opposite), complete the area above before starting the next colour block, and always maintain the direction of the stitch. The stitches of the next block of colour will either butt or slot in between the previous stitches.

- You can stitch birds with a blunt tail, such as the finch in this project, on the hoop, using the same elongated stem stitch as the rest of the bird.

- Never stitch within the eye ring or the bill.

- Long, slender tails (such as that of the fairy wren) should not be stitched on the hoop. Instead, paint it in the required colour using acrylic paint. Once dry, cut out with the bird and stitch it into place on the work using a slanted satin stitch with a single strand of stranded cotton. It is sometimes helpful to begin by using angled guide stitches on either side of the tail to attach it to the work, giving a central line similar to the shaft of a feather.

- Use only solid colours, as any shading is added as necessary with straight stitch, following the lines and shape of the bird. Some shading (from light to dark) will occur naturally when the bird is padded as it is applied to the work.

- Complete all of the birds to be used and store them flat, in separate envelopes, until you are ready to apply them to the background, as described on pages 94–95.

Partially finished finch on the hoop.

Changing colour blocks

There are two methods: blending and butting.

Blending

A smooth and gradual change from one colour into another. Using elongated stem stitch, stitch to the start of the next colour to be used. Turn and continue stitching the colour block to as far as needed leaving an irregular edge. You will find this occurs naturally. See A on the example to the right.

Thread up the next colour and begin stitching at the top of the block by slotting the stitch into the gaps left; it is not necessary to place them exactly into the stitch holes left by the previous block. B shows this; with some shading along the back of the bird.

Butting

Butting one block of colour up against another involves using the same stitch as above. The difference is that at the point of colour change, all stitches will end on the same line, so that it become a distinct change. This will mean filling in at each turn.

Begin with the next colour with the stitches butting against the last, again filling the edge as needed. This is shown in example C here. With both it is important to maintain the direction of the stitches.

Stitched sampler, showing colour changes

A *Irregular edge finish – ready for blending of edge.*

B *Blending of two colours.*

C *Butted joining of colours.*

D *This shows the approach needed for the finches in the project. In each case the body is blended, while the eyepatch is butted.*

All examples are stitched using two stands of stranded cotton. The finch in this example is stitched with two strands. Compare it with the same bird from the project (below), which is stitched with one strand. The finch in the example above is slightly bulky in comparison.

Detailing birds

Besides small patches, streaks or bars of contrasting colour on wings, chest, tails and other parts of birds' bodies, many birds exhibit details that are critical to a realistic appearance: the speckling of a hatchling; the colour morphing of a goshawk; the rictal bristles of the butcher bird; the hackles of the raven or eagle; or the nuptial plumes of the egret – to mention just a few. These small but important details are left until last, as it is simpler to overstitch the basic colour blocks of the body.

To add these details, we use a single strand of the required colour, weaving it through the back of the work and bringing it up at the longest point of a change, such as a patch. Using a satin stitch, you can then fill in the area over the top of the base stitches, making sure the stitches are in line. Finish each patch before moving on to the left, and refer to your notes and drawings as needed.

A typical example is the finely barred breast of the black and white double-barred finch, where the base colour would be white and the black bars over-stitched one bar at a time.

Preparing the birds to be applied

As a general rule, check the order in which the birds are to be applied to the background and position each bird in place. Any bird that overlaps others should be applied last. Check the placement of the birds against the tacked areas and perches and adjust as needed.

For this project, the birds are stitched in the following order – the top one, the bottom one, then the middle bird which lies over both (see pages 74–75).

1 To prepare the birds, cut a rectangular piece of Vliesofix to completely cover each bird. Place the bird face-down on a soft pad, with the Vliesofix section glue-side down over the bird.

2 Iron using a hot iron with a dry setting. Should there be any sign of scorching, use an ironing cloth. Lift the corner of the Vliesofix paper to make sure the glue has taken and has a slightly clear 'rubbery' feel. If not, re-iron.

3 Remove the Vliesofix paper backing and use very sharp embroidery scissors to carefully cut away all remaining calico at the very edge of the stitching, leaving any underlap sections in place. These will be stitched to the background: there is no turning allowance.

4 Make the bill using a suitably-coloured leather or suede. Use sticky tape to secure a tracing of the beak, with an allowance to go under the bird's head, to a small piece of the leather. Cut along the outline, making sure the eye space is not covered by the bill's allowance.

5 Thread up a fine needle with the same colour polycotton and take a few stitches into the back of the head, position the bill into place and stitch to hold it in place.

6 Finish all birds to this point. Using a pair of tweezers, place the birds into position over the background, making sure that any necessary adjustments are noted. To protect the stitched edge, put each into a separate envelope – the less you handle it, the better.

Two of the birds stitched into place, ready for the third to be applied.

Applying the birds

In this example, the first and second finches are already stitched in place, as shown to the right. This sequence looks at how the third is added.

1 Thread a no. 9 crewel needle with a single strand of the same coloured thread used on the bird. Starting where the bill joins at the top of the head, begin to apply the bird using a modified stem stitch. Always bring the needle up in the background layers at the very edge of the bird's body and take it down through the edge of the body.

2 Stitch to the end of the body (usually the wing or rump), changing thread colours as needed. Adjust the stitch angle and size so that they conform to the bird's body without disturbing the layers of stitches.

3 Gently but lightly begin to stuff the bird with wadding (batting) to the stitched line. Stitch under the chin and throat towards the belly, then add further wadding to the head area. Continue stitching and adjusting the wadding in the chest and belly area until completed.

4 Stitch the tail but do not stuff. Stitch the bill down into the head area; begin at the junction of the bill to hold it in place first. Put a small one-wrap knot in place for the nostril and then run the needle through the undersurface of the leather and catch the point of the beak to the background if needed.

5 Finally stitch along the wing line using an open back stitch rather than a straight stitch, as this will lock the wing into place. Pull the surface of the bird down to mould the stuffing and give contour to the wing, but do not pull tightly or firmly – gently does it. It is important not to over-stuff the bird.

6 At this point we add the eyes. I use small teddy bear eyes, 2 or 3mm (⅛in) in size depending on the size of the bird itself. Those with a round open shank are the best. Stitch around the eye ring, pulling it firmly down to the base fabric. Next, gently squeeze the shank of the eye into an oval shape, making sure the needle will fit through.

7 Remove everything from the frame: Use a stiletto to carefully punch a hole through the eye ring, then position the eye by pushing the shank through the hole.

8 Turn the whole frame over while holding the eye in place. With a pair of forceps, grip and gently bend the shank so that it lies relatively flat against the base fabric, then stitch it into place through the shank. Turn the frame over and back into position.

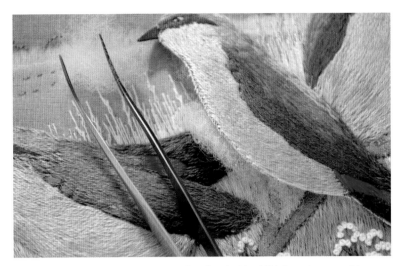

Step 3: Stitching and stuffing. The wadding (batting) is visible here. I use an old rounded envelope opener to adjust the stuffing.

Step 5: All finches stitched to the work.

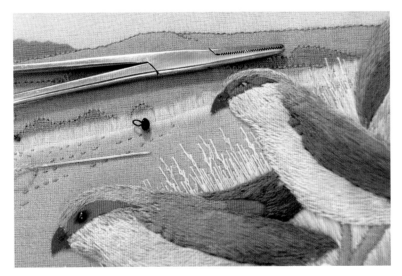

Step 6: Preparing to add the eye to the third bird.

Adding legs and claws

Once secured to the surface, you can add the birds' claws and legs. The foot in most birds usually has four digits or toes, each with a hooked claw, and is commonly called the claw. There are three sections to a bird's leg: the muscular femur, which is often covered and hidden by feathers; the tibiotarsus, being the most obvious, is usually called the leg; and the foot. The approach to stitching these differs slightly depending on the bird's posture, as described below:

Do check the colour of the legs. The colour of legs and bills will change to a darkish colour when the bird dies. Because of subtle changes during surface stitching, the position of the legs often changes and you could find a need to adjust the size, angles and placement of the legs.

Example A – resting on a perch From the sides of the body, make three straight stitches, all slightly apart and in the same direction. Beginning with the central stitch, couch each into a gentle curve and place a tiny stitch indicating a claw on each. If necessary, add a few stitches from the body to indicate fluffed-out feathers.

Examples B and C – perched From the lower part of the belly, make a long straight stitch to the end of the central claw (see right, (i)). Making the stitch slightly shorter, repeat on either side for claws two and three (ii). Gently couch the claws into place (iii), then bring the needle up at the body of the bird and wrap the three stitches together to a little above the curves of the claw (iv).

Give the thread a gentle tug to even out the wraps and stitch into place. Visualize the angle of the femur and bring the needle up a short distance from the body. Couch the top of the leg into place. Finish with a French knot on the outer point to form the joint. Finally, if needed, make a small stitch for the back claw.

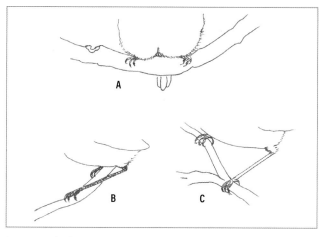

Legs and claws

When the bird is settled low on its perch all that is needed is an indication of the claw positions (A). However, when the bird is in a more upright position, the angle of the leg from the body to the perch is important, as it gives the bird movement and attitude (B and C).

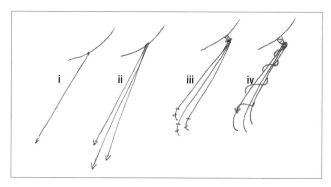

Stitch directions for perched legs.

Detail of the legs from the finished artwork.

Finishing the birds

Detail of the birds on the finished work. See pages 56–57 for the complete embroidery.

This manner of stitching is very time-consuming and can take up to eight hours to complete a small bird such as a scrub wren or a finch. The end result is a bird's body filled with densely-packed stitches flowing in a natural manner that will closely resemble the feathers.

When the stitching is completed, carefully stroke the stitch lines with the eye of a needle, this aligns the stitches and removes any dust or fluff that may have settled on the work.

Remove it from the hoop and iron face down on a soft pad. Use a hot, steam setting to iron the work.

FINISHING THE WORK

Once all the birds have been stitched into place, it is time to finish any outstanding elements such as the flowers and leaves on the shrubbery. The work is then completed.

At this point, I now place the 'window' into position over the finished work and put it in a place where I can see or catch glimpses of it during the day. I find this a particularly helpful way to ensure there is nothing else needing to be done on the work. In the case of this project, I felt the balance between the sky area and the land was too great. I could decrease the sky area by cutting some away, or I could lift the overlay and insert a section of silk paper made to resemble cloud formations. I decided that the silk paper would resolve the problem.

I occasionally use silk paper slips as a way of texturing areas on tree trunks and rock formations, as clouds of differing densities and as mist rising between tree lines and ranges. Depending on its density, it can be cut into shapes needing a sharp edge or formed into specific landscape elements. I use silk 'caps' or 'hankies' to give a soft clouded effect and silk 'tops' to give a semi-gloss and a striated effect. I recommend undyed tops and caps, but if you can find them, you can use over-dyed.

TIP

The clouds in this work were not deliberately shaped. They were made from the frayed-out subtle edges of the silk as it was laid onto the tulle in small fine sections. However, if storm or heavy clouds are needed, they can be shaped with scissors so that the edges of the heads of the clouds are distinct and the base line is subtle. Otherwise, and as seen in this work, layers can be superimposed to give depth in particular places.

PROJECT ONE

98

The completed work, ready to be mounted and framed as described on pages 142–147.
A larger version can be seen on pages 56–57.

Silk paper clouds

Being only one layer thick, the technique described here results in very fine paper that is well-suited for this subtle work. Before you begun, use the heavy-duty plastic to protect the working surface and floor. Make up the following solutions in the jars: solution 1 – one teaspoon (5ml) washing-up detergent to one litre tap water; solution 2 – equal proportions of acrylic gloss medium and tap water.

If you plan to colour or texture the silk it in any way, have the paints or inks made up into solutions ready to apply and the texture to hand.

1 Lay down one piece of tulle on the black plastic surface.

2 Begin laying the silk fibre down on the tulle as follows: carefully pull or tease out manageable sections from the silk and lay them on the tulle. Pull another section and lay it so that it slightly overlaps the first and continue until you have laid sufficient for your needs. Because you are using the paper as a slip, it will not be necessary to have more than one layer of the silk. If you are going to texture this layer with thread, do it now.

3 Cover the silk layer with the second piece of tulle.

4 Using the detergent solution, paint both sides of the silk 'sandwich'. This is important, as silk fibre repels water and by thoroughly wetting it and mopping up the surplus, it will absorb the medium easily. Use the towelling to mop up any excess.

5 If you need to colour the silk, do so now, using diluted acrylic inks. Subtle colour changes can be achieved in this way, particularly if there is no dyed silk available. The colours can lighten as they dry, so it is therefore better to do a series of colour runs.

6 Carefully paint or spray the silk on both sides with the medium. If you have used coloured silk and combined with the inks above, the colours will merge together. Mop up any excess.

7 Peg the 'sandwich', tulle only, to the drying rack or to a clothesline. Leave until completely dry. Don't be impatient, because if it is not completely dry, the tulle won't pull away cleanly on the fine edges.

8 Pull the tulle layers apart and remove one of them. Remove the silk paper by carefully pushing a finger under it and teasing the paper gently from the tulle. Your paper is ready for use. Store between acid-free tissue paper until needed.

You will need

- Heavy-duty black plastic
- Old towelling, cotton knit fabrics or sponges
- Drying rack and pegs with plastic and towels to catch the drips
- 2 x two-litre jars
- Washing-up detergent
- Acrylic gloss medium
- Two 3cm (1¼in) household paint brushes
- Two pieces of bridal tulle (lightweight net)
- Silk tops or cap
- Acrylic inks with suitable brushes to colour the silk
- Various threads for texturing (optional)

Detail of the silk paper clouds.

TIP

Silk paper can be used to construct a range of beautiful garments and other objects, such as bowls and books, using similar techniques with more layers. There are many information sheets and books on using silk paper in this way if you would like to experiment and explore.

Project Two
The Nestlings

Rose robins – *Petroica rosea*

PLANNING THE BIRD AND HABITAT

I have seen these small delicate robins in the escarpment area (part of the great dividing range of Eastern Australia) of New England National Park, near where I live in New South Wales. Rose robins are, on the whole, unobtrusive – but, once sighted, it is fascinating to watch the way they forage: flitting from a perch to snap insects in mid-air in a rolling, somersaulting flight; or plucking them from leaves before flitting back to the perch.

After breeding, the female builds a nest approximately two metres from the ground on horizontal branch junctions. The nest is a neat cup of woven fibres and moss bound together with cobwebs, lined with soft plant down and small downy feathers. She incubates her eggs alone while her mate feeds her, either on the nest or nearby while indicating their territory with a clicking sound or a low trilling call. Both feed the nestlings once hatched until they fledge.

The habitat for the rose robin is more complex than the open landscape of the tablelands and grasslands of the slopes and plains that the finches frequent. Because of the contrast and complexity, the landscape of the cool temperate rainforest around the Point Lookout area of the park became the chosen place to base the design. Point Lookout overhangs a deep, heavily-treed valley followed by line after line of tree canopies outlining the ranges as far as the eye can see – on a clear day, you can see all the way to the Pacific ocean. Clear or shrouded in mist, the Lookout is one of my favourite places.

The deep valleys of the escarpment are full of a wonderful variety of vegetation namely many different ferns, shrubs, orchids, moss and lichen-covered vines, trees, rocky ledges or huge boulders. Because of the canopies of the trees, mainly eucalyptus, there is a lack of light, a silence broken only by bird song, adding to the sense of mystery of something hidden.

The bird

Class Aves
Order Passeriformes (perching or songbirds)
Family Muscicapidae
Genus *Petroica*
Species *P. rosea*
Races 56

The rose robin belongs to the Muscicapidae family, which includes a loosely related series of songbirds – the thrushes, the flycatchers and the robins. Of these, fifteen known species are endemic to Australia. I have chosen the rose robin because its shape is so similar to the European robin, and it offers a more complex and intimate habitat than that of the finch in the earlier project.

This robin is both a climatic and an altitude migrant; breeding in the Australian summer in the cool fern-filled gullies or valleys among the tall trees of the cool temperate rain forests. In the autumn they migrate north or east to be closer to the coast and the warmer parts of the more open forests. Being solitary, they travel alone or in breeding pairs, often returning to the same breeding territory each year, where once seen are easier to find in subsequent years.

The completed work.

CREATING THE WORKING DESIGN

When I began drawing up the design, I wanted to get a sense of looking down from a high point into the depths of a fern and tree-filled gully or valley with the branches, nest and birds appearing to float across the background. The initial design was to have hand-cut fern fronds of suede superimposed across the foreground. However, the balance and contrast were way, way too heavy for the proposed embroidered midground because they altered the sense of depth and distance I wanted... Back to the drawing board!

The trees, shrubs and ferns of all the forest storeys were now to be closely stitched behind a group of lichen and moss-covered boulders leaving the branch, nest and birds in the same dominant position and the middle ground now achieving the effect I needed for the work. Much more work but a better result.

Master copy

This is presented at actual size.

Master and layout copies

The design was compiled by using a combination of several drawings, rough sketches and photographs of the area. I included the sketch of the old eucalyptus tree, which had probably been struck by lightning many years ago, as well as using the discovery of an intact but empty robin's nest in a lowish branch along one of the fern, lichen and moss-covered pathways through the area.

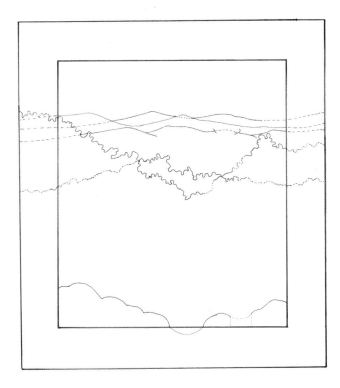

Layout copy 1 – background and window

The master copy fits within the smaller rectangle (the window). As usual, the background layers of the design are extended to the full width of the layout copy, including the mounting allowances.

Layout copy 2 – background and surface elements

This layout copy is reproduced at half actual size. Use a photocopier or scanner to enlarge it by 200 per cent, or trace the outlines from the master copy opposite. The background elements are labelled BE 8–11, as explained on page 106. The surface elements are labelled SE 12–16, as explained on page 115.

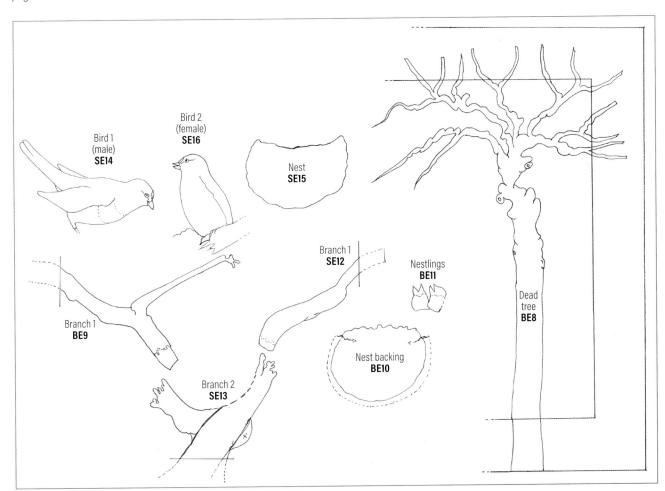

Bird 1 (male) **SE14**

Bird 2 (female) **SE16**

Nest **SE15**

Branch 1 **SE12**

Nestlings **BE11**

Dead tree **BE8**

Branch 1 **BE9**

Branch 2 **SE13**

Nest backing **BE10**

LAYERING THE BACKGROUND

As you will have found with *A Brief Flash of Red*, the layering process of the background is both logical and easy. This project appears – and is – more complicated because there are two layering sequences under the overlay of silk organza.

1 The actual background layers of the landscape.

2 The landscape elements.

If necessary, refer back to pages 52 and 60 for a reminder of the fabric preparation, and have all materials and equipment on hand that will be needed to layer the background. Remember that each layer can be cut to the size needed and the edges prepared, but the profile cutting is not done until the layers are ready to be placed in order on the frame.

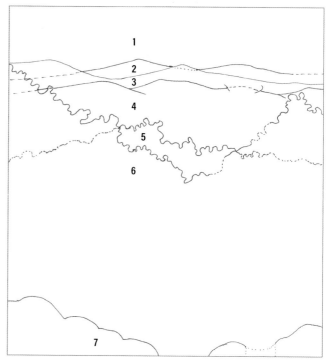

Detail of layout copy 1 noted with the order of layering

The design space holding the master copy measures 18 x 20cm (7⅛ x 7⅞in). The mounting allowance in all dimensions is 3cm (1³⁄₁₆in). The total size is 24 x 26cm (9½ x 10¼in).

Fabric preparation sheet

This gives the sizes of all layers used in the layout, and any additional preparation required for each. The background layers must include all necessary allowances. The mounting allowance in all dimensions is 3cm (1³⁄₁₆in).

Fabric	Layer	Preparation
	1 – Sky	- Sky blue cotton, 24 x 10cm (9½ x 4in) - Iron
	2 – Range 1	- Deep blue silk organza, 24 x 3.5cm (9½ x 1³⁄₈in) - Trace (see 'Tissue paper tracings' on page 61) and cut
	3 – Range 2	- Deep blue silk organza, 24 x 4cm (9½ x 1½in) - Trace and cut
	4 – Range 3	- Deep blue silk organza, 24 x 6cm (9½ x 2½in) - Trace and cut
	5 – Tree line 1	- Deep green silk organza, 18 x 5.5cm (7⅛ x 2¼in) - Cut freehand
	6 – Tree line 2	- Mix of green cotton, 24 x 20cm (9½ x 8in) - Vliesofix, cut freehand
	7 – Boulders	- Mix of grey cotton, 19 x 4cm (7½ x 1½in) - Trace, Vliesofix and cut

Background layer placement

Place the prepared frame on the worktable and position the window tool centrally on the calico. Pull it forward on the frame so that the outer edge of the base of the window is resting on the internal edge of the frame. This central placement is important in maintaining an equal tension when stitching.

You will need

- The prepared fabrics ready to cut or fray and layer
- Rigid frame and clamps – laced and ready
- Window tool
- Scissors
- Pins
- Tweezers
- Small ruler

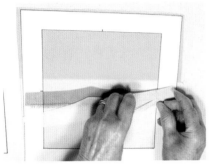

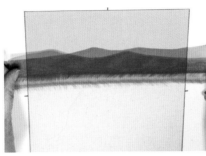

Note how the tone builds up gradually with repeated layers of the same colour.

1 Pick up layer 1 (sky) and place it over the window so that all allowances are covered. Carefully remove the window, then replace it in position over the sky layer; there should be a sliver of the sky fabric at the top and side edges of the fabric showing. From this point on, all following layers are superimposed upon the previous layer. Add layers 2, 3 and 4 (the three range layers) in turn, one after the other.

2 Add layer 5 (tree line 1) in the same way.

3 Next, add the foreground: layer 6 (tree line 2), followed by layer 7 (boulders).

4 The layered background is now complete. Carefully remove the window once more and replace it on top. The sequence continues on page 107.

Landscape elements layer placement

As before, use ink to trace all of the background elements onto tissue paper, then tape them to fabric and cut them out.

Fabric preparation sheet

This gives the sizes of all layers used in the layout, and any additional preparation required for each. The background layers must include all necessary allowances.

Fabric	Layer	Preparation
	8 – Dead tree	- Grey suede, 26 x 18cm (10¼ x 7⅛ in) - See page 67 for notes on suede
	9 – Left tree branch	- Cream suede, 11 x 8cm (4⅜ x 3⅛ in) - See page 67 for notes on suede
	10 – Nest backing	- Brown silk organza, 5 x 7cm (2 x 2¾in) - N/A
	11 – Nestlings	- Brown silk organza, 3 x 4cm (1¼ x 1½in) - N/A
	12 – Overlay	- White silk organza, 24.5 x 26cm (9½ x 10¼in) - Iron

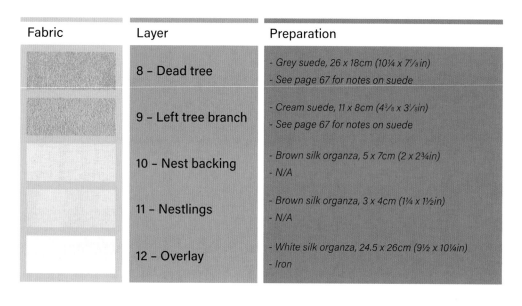

Detail of the background elements

These details of layout copy 2 (see page 103) show just the background elements. The numbering relates to the layer.

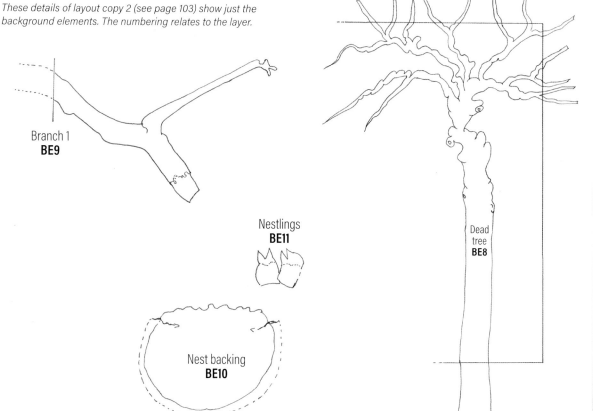

Branch 1
BE9

Nestlings
BE11

Nest backing
BE10

Dead tree
BE8

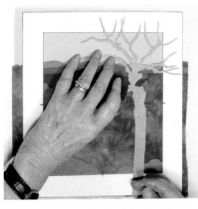

5 Place layer 8 (the dead tree) in place. Note that it overlaps the window as shown in the diagram opposite.

6 Place card silhouettes (see page 39) of the the surface branches to help with layering the left-hand branch.

7 Remove the window and position the left-hand branch, using the silhouettes to help you. Remove the card silhouettes and place the overlay on top.

8 Turn back the overlay, being careful not to dislodge the branch. Position the nest backing, then place the nestlings on top.

TIP

The process for making a stitched nest off-frame is looked at in more detail on page 127.

9 Replace the overlay to complete the layering. All the background elements are now in place, ready to back stitch.

BACK STITCHING

The back stitching of the landscape layers is essentially the same as in the first project with one difference: the number of tree lines stitched. If in doubt, refer to pages 70–71.

Back stitch work plan

Using a no. 9 crewel needle and a single strand of DMC 3022 stranded cotton throughout, work your back stitch according to the order of layering. Remember to stitch the indentations of the tree line of the first layer, and any design lines drawn in others.

The background layers

You will notice from the image that there are several tree lines stitched between tree line 1 and into range line 3. This gives the illusion that there are many trees and valleys without having other layers of fabric to stitch through.

Note that the back stitching must follow the order of work below, which is not the same as the earlier order of layering. Also, look at the way the tree line layers have been cut. Layer 6 from earlier is back stitched first; and layer 5 is back stitched second. As stated earlier, always back stitch from the lowest cut layer towards the top of the work (this is usually a tree layer – in this case, tree line 1).

1 Back stitch tree line 1. Beginning at the centre and work out to the mounting allowance; return to the centre and work out to the other side. Stitch the indentations as needed for both interest and to stabilize the layer.

2 Back stitch tree line 2. Start from the side you are most comfortable stitching.

3 Stitch range line 3. Range line 4 is optional. Do not stitch the last range line.

Back stitching order of work

1 – Tree line 2

2 – Tree line 1

3 – Range line 3

(4) – Range line 2 (optional)

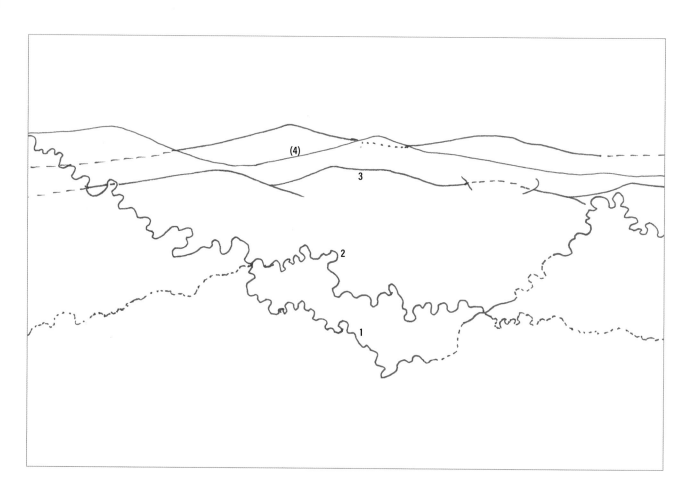

The landscape elements

In this project, the landscape elements are the tree branch, nest and nestlings, and the dead tree (see page 106). Off-frame stitching and application of natural elements is described in further detail in the next chapter if you need additional guidance.

When back stitching a line that continues under an element (for example the dead tree), stitch to the edge of the element, then bring the thread up on the other side of the element before continuing stitching as needed. There is no need to end off and start again.

4 Back stitch the left tree branch (BE9) using a single strand of DMC 3790.

5 Back stitch the dead tree (BE8), using a single strand of DMC 3787. Detail the tree using the same thread with two strands.

6 Back stitch the top edge of the nest backing (BE10) using a single strand of DMC 3790.

7 Back stitch the nestlings using a single strand of DMC 3790.

TIP

Back stitch progression is explained in more detail on page 121, if you need help back stitching the tree.

Enlarged detail of the left-hand branch being back stitched on frame.

SURFACE STITCHING

Having completed the back stitching, check the frame to see if it needs to be re-tensioned. If so, re-tension it as explained on page 19. Once the tension is correct, proceed with the on-frame surface stitching before moving on to the off-frame surface stitching.

The foreground in this project is heavily stitched to represent the depth and sense of hidden mystery of a cool temperate rainforest. All forests are divided into three main parts:

Upper storey Involves the canopies of the tall trees of the forest.

Middle storey The shrubbery and fern tree species and orchids.

Lower storey The ferns, lilies, orchids, mosses and lichens.

On-frame surface stitching

In all parts of the forest, and particularly in the middle and lower storeys, there is a confusing complexity of intermingled floral species which are depicted with a variety of simple stitches:

Adapted feather stitch Structures of trees and shrubs. See page 77 for the technique.

Stacked fly stitches Background tree fern growth and tree fern.

French knots Shrubbery flora and leaves. Lichen and moss patterns.

Detached chain stitches Ferns of lower storey.

You will need

Number of strands of DMC stranded cotton – one or two strands.

EUCALYPTUS FOREST
- Structures 3787
- Canopy 3346 + 936
- New growth 920 + 3346

SHRUBBERY
- Tree fern trunk 839 + 3790
- Dead fronds 3826
- Ferns 3363 + 3047 + 3790 + 3826
- Shrub structure 3790
- Shrub leaves 3346
- Shrub flowers 3346 + 746 or 3024
- Lower fern fronds 3790, 703 + 704

BOULDERS
- Moss 704
- Lichen 3024, 3052, 780

SUEDE BRANCH
- Over-stitched with 842, 3790

Threads for the background.

The foreground surface stitchery

The foreground is stitched from beneath the lowest back stitched line to the base line, as described in the work plan overleaf works through the foreground step by step.

Use the master copy (see page 102) with the map of stitched foreground elements (see page 113) for placement. Stitching in this order saves the thread or arm brushing across the stitches and disturbing them.

This detail shows some of the foreground stitchery. Although it appears complex, all can be achieved with just a few stitches.

Work plan for on-frame surface stitching

1 - Preparation Start by placing the cut-outs of the birds, tree branches and nest into place and tack around them to give you the approximate placement of these elements before you begin the surface stitching of the middle ground. You don't stitch into these areas, so the silhouettes help.

2 - Upper storey This is stitched from below, following the back stitched tree lines with the trunk, falling to approximately the boulder line with the eucalyptus trees. The trees are stitched in the same manner as those shown on the sampler for the first project (see page 80).

The trees have the coloured flashes of 'new growth' along the canopies. The trunks extend close to the top edge of the boulder line. Note that many of the trunks will be over-stitched as the work progresses.

3 - Middle storey This section contains the tree fern, tree fern fronds, fern fronds and shrubbery. These are stitched in the following order, from beneath the eucalyptus tree canopies and from branches to the boulder edges. Refer to the map opposite throughout.

- Stitch the shrubbery structure areas. The techniques are the same as in the first project (see pages 86–87).

- Stitch the tree fern trunk as shown on the right side of the work using a series of irregular satin stitch (see page 156). Use the brown threads (839 + 3790).

- Work the tree fern fronds using stacked fly stitches (see page 156) as described below, with two differing greens that form a canopy by angling the fronds towards the top of the trunk, and finishing with a few central French knots. Add a couple of dead fronds towards the base for contrast.

- Ferns – group 1a. These are stitched from the nest area and its branch to the isolating stitch on the left side, then downwards to the boulders. Fill the area completely, with the exception of the shrubbery structures.

- Ferns – group 1b. On the right, these are stitched between the large branch and the dead tree to the isolating stitch, filling the complete area apart from the stitched fronds and the fern tree trunk. The stitches are slotted into the tree's canopies and the shrubbery as needed.

- Stitch the shrubbery leaves and flowers over the structures using 2-wrap French knots. Stitch the leaves first using angled straight stitches into the lines of the structures, then insert the flowers among them to completely cover the structures and blend them into the surrounding ferns.

4 - Lower storey This is the section that forms the forest floor and the foreground of the work. It contains the ferns, mosses and lichens of the boulder layer of the foreground. Stitch in the following order:

- **Ferns** These are stitched over the bases of the previous ferns and eucalyptus tree trunks using the technique in the box below.

- **Moss** Using French knots and the same bright green threads as the ferns, stitch the moss closely along the edges and into the shapes that form the boulders. Scatter small shapes and single knots around the lichen, too.

- **Lichen** The variety used in the work is known as a crustose, which is a low grey-green species that fades, during dry times, to grey. It grows in a spreading circular pattern with a central terracotta fruiting body. Use the master copy (see page 102) to help with the placement of the stitched groups.

5 - Suede branch The left branch is suede, layered beneath the silk organza, which knocks it back a little too much. To give it more emphasis, use elongated stem stitch (see page 156), to work over the branch. This gives a similar appearance to the right side of the branch (see page 111) which had been stitched off-frame, but is lower in profile.

Middle storey fern technique

For the ferns and fern fronds in the middle storey, use fly stitch as closely stacked blocks to represent the many ferns growing within this landscape. The stacks begin with either a small straight stitch or a detached chain stitch with fly stitches around it. The stacks can be irregular in length but equal in width.

Use a no. 9 crewel needle with a single strand of DMC stranded cotton with a mix of colours (alternatively, you can find or over-dye a thread with harmonious colours). I worked this area using a variegated silk thread; however, it can be done using four needles, each threaded with a separate colour. Working in this way means that the colours can be quickly and easily interchanged.

Lower storey fern technique

Thread two bright contrasting greens using two strands of stranded cotton, one of each, on a no. 9 crewel needle. The stitches making up the frond are placed at an angle to the guideline, opposite each other finishing at the upper edge of the boulders. Start by making a series of slightly angled straight stitches, each 1–2cm (3/8–3/4in) long and approximately 0.5cm (1/4in) apart, using a single strand of DMC 3790 forming central guidelines.

The stitch forming the leaflets is detached chain (see page 155). The thread is brought up at the top of the guide stitch, then taken down at the same point and brought up at the required length in the loop to form a catch stitch taken into the guidelines to form the leaf. The stitches are placed at an angle to the guidelines opposite each other and finish at the edge of the boulders.

The silhouette outlines need to be tacked into place prior to beginning the surface stitching.

Map of the stitched foreground elements

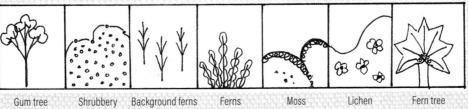

| Gum tree | Shrubbery | Background ferns | Ferns | Moss | Lichen | Fern tree |

Off-frame stitchery

There are more off-frame elements to be worked in this project than *A Brief Flash of Red*. Not only do the robins show a distinct difference in colouration between the male and female, which is not present in the finches, there is also the branch, made up of three sections, upon which a nest is positioned.

The off-frame elements can be worked on a hoop when and in whatever order you prefer. When each is completed, remove it from the hoop and prepare the element so that it is ready to be positioned on the background. Keep them in a clear envelope for protection and apply them in the order given below.

Pages 90–95 cover all the areas related to stitching, preparing and applying the birds and branches to the work. In particular, page 94 details how to prepare the birds for application to the work. The stitch used for both the birds and branches is, as in the first project, elongated stem stitch (see page 156).

Work plan for off-frame stitching

1 – Male bird (SE14) The male bird is stitched and applied in the same way as the finches.

2 – Branch 1 (SE12) The branches are stitched and applied in much the same way as the birds. There is more information on the specifics of the technique on page 121.

3 – Branch 2 (SE13)

4 – Nest (SE15) Being cup-shaped, the top of the nest requires the background element of silk organza, of a related colour, cut to shape and layered into place. The same applies to the nestlings. The off-frame stitching of the nest is described on page 117.

5 – Tree trunk base is completed.

6 – Female bird (SE16) This is stitched and applied over both the nest and branch.

7 – Legs or claws These are stitched when all the elements are in place.

You will need

Number of strands of DMC stranded cotton – one or two strands.

MALE BIRD
- Head, throat, back, wings and tail 535
- Breast 3608
- Belly to rump, under tail, patch above bill blanc white

FEMALE BIRD
- Patch above bill 746
- Head, back, wing 3032
- Chevron patches on wing 3047
- Cheek 762
- Chest into belly (for shading) 3047, 746

FEATURES
- Legs 3787
- Bills black leather
- Eye for male black 3mm (⅛in) teddy bear eye
- Eye for female – oval bead painted black

BRANCHES (TWO SURFACE ELEMENTS)
- Branch 1 (right – SE12) 842; details 3790
- Branch 2 (central – SE13) 3790; details 3781
- Nest (SE15) overdyed silk bouclé or 3032, 3790, 762
- Mixed greens 3347, 3348, 320, 581

BACKGROUND TREES
- Lower trunk – fine strips of brown suedes with orange and black beads

Threads for the birds.

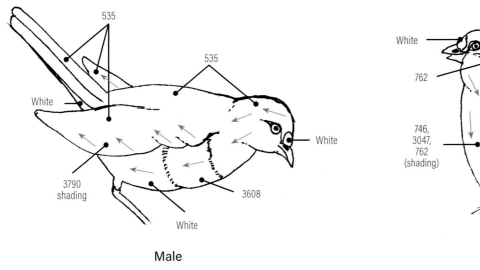

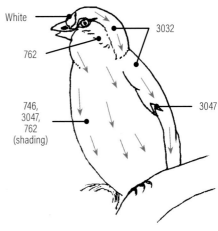

Male

Female

The planned stitch direction and DMC thread colours are noted here.

Surface elements details

These details of layout copy 2 (see page 103) show just the surface elements. The numbering relates to the order of work opposite.

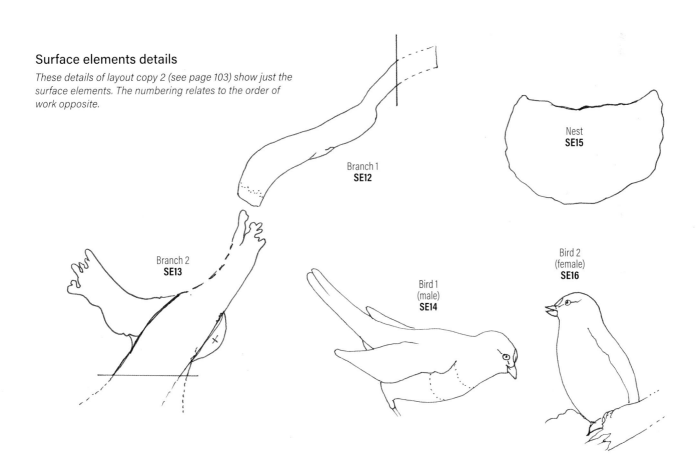

Branch 1
SE12

Nest
SE15

Branch 2
SE13

Bird 1
(male)
SE14

Bird 2
(female)
SE16

3787

3022

Branch L
842
3033

3790
+
The end of the
branch is left until
the bird's beak is
in position.

Trees
Trunk –3787
Canopy –
936 + 3346
920 + 3363
Small shrub
3347 + 1 +746

Fern tree
581 + 3347

Ferns
Look up 703

Rocks and lichen
3363 + 762

Grass
1: 3776

Work in progress

The birds and branches stitched to the work, with the nest about to be added. You'll see my working notes on the frame.

The nest

As shown on the facing page, an organza nest shape has already been created as part of creating the background (see page 107). Note that an outline of the nestlings has been placed in order to ensure the heads will be visible once the stitched nest is placed into position. We now need to create the nest to fit.

Creating the stitched nest

Start by tracing the nest shape from the Master copy (see page 102) onto calico. Draw in the stitch direction. Because the nest is three-dimensional, the direction should either follow the outer shape or curve diagonally, but not horizontally across the body of the nest. Prepare the materials to be used.

Closely couch overdyed silk bouclé at a slightly curved diagonal line across the shape, with a single strand of DMC 3032. Finish it with two lines of stem stitch around the rim of the nest.

Outline the top of the nest's underlayer with a mix of back stitch and small one-wrap knots. Use seed stitch to fill the area within using the same colours as the greens of the nest.

When all the stitching is complete, the nest is treated in the same way as the birds: Vliesofixed and the calico removed, as described on pages 94–95. Place it safely in an envelope until ready to be stitched into position.

Stitching the nest into place

Although the nest is finished as for the bird, it is applied to the work slightly differently:

1 Cut and tack a small layer of stuffing to the back of the finished nest. Stitch tiny down feathers into place so that they will slightly encroach onto the female's belly.

2 Position the nest and stitch it into place with small open back stitches through the body of the nest to flatten it slightly. Next, stitch the edge into place in an open but similar way to a bird.

3 Finally, gently tease out the loops of the bouclé onto the branch.

Detail of the stitching
This detail shows the stitched nest, ready to be applied.

FINISHING THE WORK

Once all of the off-frame elements have been applied, the final checks are made to the work. Check whether any filling-in is needed surrounding any surface work, and check all of the elements. Stitch if needed.

At this point, I couched a worm into place in the male's beak. The worm is a very small piece of silk chenille thread, with two tiny French knots for its eyes.

The completed work, ready to be mounted and framed as described on pages 142–147. A larger version can be seen on page 101.

Detail of the worm.

The rose robins' nest is a cup-shaped nest of moss, lichen, plant fibre bound together with cobwebs, with a woven appearance.

Natural elements of a landscape

There are many natural elements within a landscape associated with birds and their habitats. These can include hollows in trees and branches, old fence posts, water holes and dripping taps, crevasses in rock faces and ledges in caves, leaves and petals, grass clumps and insects. All add to the complexity of the stitched habitat, creating further techniques, the use of different fabrics and threads and can include using one or another of the following techniques. This chapter explores them in more detail so you can apply them to your own future work.

Elements drawn or traced and painted onto a background fabric

1 Using a light box or a backlit window, trace the element – a branch, in this example – from the layout copy for your project onto the appropriate piece of background fabric (this will depend on the project, but will usually be the sky), extending it into the mounting allowance as necessary. Alternatively, you can paint freehand directly onto the fabric.

2 Tape the fabric to a piece of heavy plastic and attach it to a board or a table.

3 Dilute acrylic paint with water to a creamy consistency. With a fine brush, such as a 0, paint the outline of the branch. This will help seal the fibres of the outline and help prevent paint running into the fabric.

4 Fill in the rest of the branch using a thicker brush and paint in details such as old branch gnarls and hollows, if needed, with a darker colour and the finer brush.

Acrylic paint scorches easily, so place an ironing cloth over the painted areas before ironing to fix the paint.

Should there be more than one element, such as tree trunks, branches or leaves, choose one or more that appear dominant and back stitch the outlines. Back stitching an element will allow it to advance from those that are not stitched, giving depth to the work.

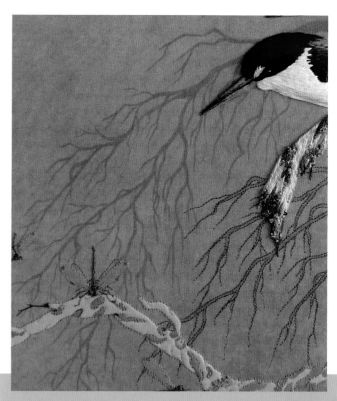

Detail from Jewels of the Forest – The Forest Kingfisher

The fine branches here have been painted directly onto the background. You can see here how the branches have been treated in three different ways depending on whether they are in the foreground, midground or background. This creates an impression of distance. The full artwork can be seen on page 15.

The cut-outs: layered background elements

Elements using this technique are cut out and become part of the layered background under the silk organza overlay. The tracings and the fabrics to be used are prepared and taped together beforehand and cut out and layered into place when needed.

It is important to decide which fabrics are to be used, as the placement of these elements give further depth and distance to the elements behind. The painted elements of the previous technique would appear to be the most distant; followed in this order: from the finest, Vliesofixed fabric, Ultrasuede and fabric Vliesofixed to fine felt. The latter would appear to be the closest.

It is also important to examine the tree's structure. After deciding on the order, number the trunk and branches in the order that they are to be back stitched. This will help prevent puckering occurring between the branches. The stitching outlines the trunk and the branches and will indicate any lines where both join together.

Regardless of the simplicity or complexity of the trunk and branches, the technique remains the same:

- Always begin close to the centre of the element and stitch towards the top and side edges of the work, adding a further 1–2cm (⅜–¾in) into the mounting allowance if necessary.

- Using the diagram (right), begin at the centre of the trunk (1) and work up to the junction of the first right-hand branch (2). Stitch the branch completely, then stitch each branch as numbered.

- The stitching is always done in two journeys. The first journey alternates from one side of an element to the other approximately every 2cm (¾in), taking the thread under the element, bringing it up and stitching a further 2cm (¾in) on the opposite side and repeating this sequence until finished. The second or return journey fills in the gaps left by the first.

- If sections of the stitching are not alternated, the fabric of the trunk or branch will move away from the stitched line, leaving a very noticeable gap, which is difficult, if not impossible, to change.

- Stitch any indentations as the work proceeds. When all the top branches are completed, work the trunk in the same manner down towards the base line and a further 2cm (¾in) into the mounting allowance.

Further detailing is usually in the form of adding knots and stitched lines for hollows and branchlets. Apart from these simple details, it is better to leave the more detailed and textural work of bark ribbons on the trunks until the foreground surface stitchery is completed. This can involve the use of small sections and strips of Ultrasuede, silk bouclé, chenille and heavier pearl cottons to be couched or held into place with French knots, or simple stitches and tiny beads.

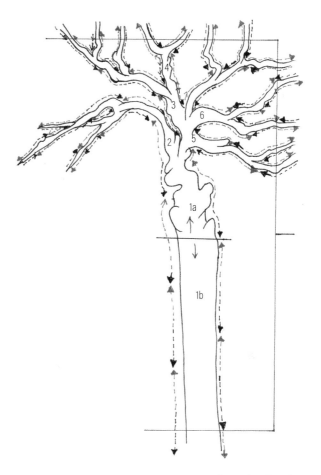

Back stitch progression of a dead tree

I am using the dead eucalyptus tree from The Nestlings *as an example for back stitching a complex element.*

The first journey is shown in red ink lines and arrows.

The second journey is shown in blue ink lines and arrows.

You can see the completed trunk of the dead tree on page 119.

Surface elements: constructed, stitched and applied

These elements can include leaves (this process would be particularly fitting for a long gum leaf or similar), petals and grass blades cut from Ultrasuede or two layers of fabric Vliesofixed together.

Distorting elements

To begin, take ink tissue tracings from the design, tape them to the fabric and cut them out. The cut element is then applied to the work using back stitch along the central vein. Only the upper levels of a grouping should be distorted during application.

1   Position the leaf into place and make a group of up to seven small back stitches along the central vein from the top.

2   Pull the end of the leaf to one or other sides and make another group of small back stitch aligning them with the first group.

3   Bring the leaf back to the original position; make another group of stitches which will lock the element into position and give a curve to the edge.

4   Should the leaf need further distortion, repeat the above sequence by pulling the end of the leaf to the opposite side and stitch as before. This will result in a curve towards the other side of the leaf.

Another way to lock these curves into place is to make a tiny French knot to the body of the leaf below or to the curved side of the leaf. Should the leaf be shorter and need further veins (an ivy leaf, for example), begin at the top and stitch in a straight line towards the point of the leaf. Return to the top, close to the first line of stitches, take two to three small stitches at a slight angle and pull the side of the leaf in towards the central vein and stitch down as before. Repeat on the other side.

Detail from Sipping Nectar – Eastern Spinebill

The grevillea leaves of this work demonstrate the distorting technique. Note how it causes the leaves to curl in a naturalistic fashion. The finished artwork can be seen on page 139.

NATURAL ELEMENTS OF A LANDSCAPE

Lacing an element over card

This technique has not been used in either of the projects in the book, but it is useful to know. For this technique, the element (such as a branch) is stitched in the same way as above. Note that any detailing must have been fully completed before you begin; and that it is difficult to stitch through card!

The main challenge of this technique is keeping the two sections aligned, particularly with a curved branch. Sometimes flowerhead pins can be helpful as they lie flat, bringing the back of the stitched surface to the felt – otherwise it is down to perseverance (or a small dab of glue on the allowances as the lacing proceeds). If used, make sure the glue has dried before applying the piece to the work.

1   Remove the completed work from the hoop, iron it and take a photocopy. When stitching on the hoop, the stitching often changes the shape and size of the piece slightly. The photocopy will give you an accurate outline from which to work.

2   Trace the outline onto firm card and use a knife to cut the element out. If necessary, cut 2mm (1/16in) from each end of the card so that it does not encroach into the mounting allowance.

3   Cut 1mm (1/32in) from the inside edge of the outline on either side to allow room for the stitched edge to roll over the card with little loss of size.

4   Use a glue stick to glue the right side of the card. Iron a piece of fine felt onto the card's surface. Carefully cut away the excess.

5   Cut the stitched branch from the calico with a 1–1.5cm (3/8–1/2in) allowance on each side, extending into the mounting allowances. Do not Vliesofix the work. Place the felt side of the card into place over the back of the stitched branch ready to begin lacing using a fine, strong thread.

6   Begin at the centre of the branch and lace from side to side clipping into any curves as needed to allow the stitching to lie flat against the card. Finish at the end of the card, overlap and stitch the mounting allowance sides together.

7   Return to the centre and stitch to the other side finishing in the same way.

Applying the finished piece to the work   Check its position, particularly the ends, to make sure the card has not extended into the allowance and that the calico ends do. Beginning at the centre using a matching colour thread, stitch it into place by bringing the needle up through the back of the work at the edge of the element at an angle and down through the element's edge at the same angle so that no stitch is visible. Alternating on either side, these stitches are only needed to anchor the element into place and therefore, need not be close to each other. Finally, stitch the calico ends into place on the allowance.

Off-frame: hand-stitched large branches and application to work

The branch in *The Nestlings* is made up of three sections, and covers all but one of the three ways of stitching, applying or mounting these types of elements. All the sections were stitched using elongated stem stitch (see page 156) in the same manner as the birds, and other stitches such as French knots for detailing.

The first section, the upper left-hand side, is a back-stitched underlay, which is then over-stitched with elongated stem stitch. The second section, on the right-hand side, is stitched off-frame using the same colours as on the left. It was stitched following the direction of the inner curve of the branch and stitched into place on the work using the tacking (basting) as a guide. The third section, the central and main parts of the branch, is stitched in two directions, giving the appearance of one branch joining another.

1 Trace the surface elements (branches 1 and 2) from the master or layout copy of the design and extend the shape into the mounting allowances.

2 Using an ink pen, trace the extended shape onto calico, noting where the mounting allowances begin, the directional arrows and an arrow at the top of the work, then tension onto a suitable size hoop. Stitch element 1 (right-hand side).

3 As element 2 is stitched in two directions, completely stitch one section before moving on to the other. Stitch the element using one or two strands of stranded cotton, keeping in mind the need to extend the stitches into the allowances by up to 2–3mm (⅛in) to allow for any shrinkage that could occur.

4 Once the element is completed with the main colour, the details and shading are then stitched using knots and straight stitches and, if needed, small sections of Ultrasuede.

5 When complete, the element is prepared and applied to the work in the same way as the birds. Note that the branches are not padded. Once stitched into place, further detailing – including any shading – can be added.

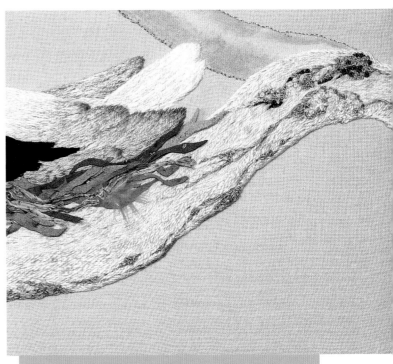

Detail from Nesting – Black Shouldered Kite

Using the off-frame hand-stitching method gives a higher profile to the element than a cut out, as well as balance and depth to the work when finished, as can be seen in this example. The finished piece can be seen on page 135.

This detail shows the branches from The Nestlings, *having been applied to the work and overstitched.*

Nests

Small birds are the masters of camouflage and concealment, building or weaving their nests in dense vegetation using related materials. Nests are often revealed after the autumn leaves have fallen and its occupants flown.

Larger birds rely less on secrecy and more on the inaccessibility of tall trees, hollows and the crevasses of cliff faces, the open spaces making it easier for the occupant to observe approaching dangers.

The materials used for nest building are readily available within the bird's specific habitat. The sticks, bark and palm leaf strips, grasses and strands are woven or stitched, bound with spiderweb or saliva. They can be lined with downy small feathers, leaf down, cobweb, fur and wool left on barbed-wire fences. Some are decorated with lichen, small petals and moss.

Some nests are no more than a scrap in sand or grass – plovers and emus. Some fill the hollows of tree trunks or branches – the parrots and cockatoos. Others are on rocky ledges – kestrels, gannets, cormorants and eagle owls – or are found at the end of a scraped tunnel – pardalotes and kingfishers.

Some nests are platforms on boggy places – brolgas and swans. Some float on water – grebes and swamp hens. Some on horizontal branches – frogmouth and crested pigeon.

Some birds weave or stitch their nests into specific shapes: the cup shape of robins; the wine glass of fantails; the dome shape of scrub wrens and grass finches; or the suspended 'purse' of a mistletoe bird.

Some nests are unusual – the sand mound of the mallee fowl; the stitched nest of the taylor bird or cisticola. Some are incredibly untidy – fairy wrens and lyrebirds; others neat and compact – the robins. Some birds, like the cuckoos, makes no nests at all.

Offering shelter from wind and rain, From snakes to mammals, from birds to ants, Such are the qualities of nests – the homes of birds.

NATURAL ELEMENTS OF A LANDSCAPE

Nests and found feathers.

Research

Research the bird's specific nest type. Ask yourself whether it is a woven or a platform nest; a neat rounded cup shape with a solid wall, or perhaps domed with a side entry. Does it appear to be simply thrown together as an untidy heap?

How is it attached? Has it been woven over thin branchlets on the outer edges of a canopy or is it cemented over a larger horizontal branch? Is it a platform floating in water, or is it one built into a natural hollow on a branch or cliff face?

Designing the nest

The shape of the nest and the materials used often indicate the bird species; therefore, if a nest is to be a part of the design, it is important that that it is specific to the bird.

Birds that build nests that are scrapes, hollows and tunnels require little work other than a physical indication during drawing up of the design and layering of the crevasse of a rock face or hole in a tree branch or trunk. Because these nests often have no visible signs, it could be the attitude and placement of the birds, food in their beaks or a wisp of building material at the entrance indicating a nest site.

It is the platform and woven nests that will need adapted materials.

Woven nests

This spinebill nest is a good example of a woven nest. It forms a distinct three-dimensional shape, and is best worked off-frame. A real spinebill nest is visible in the top right of the picture on the opposite page.

Platform nests

A platform nest with an eagle chick. Platform nests are typically relatively large and fairly flat, with little more than a depression to give them shape.

Birds and bananas: decorating nests

Crimson finches build the most incredibly untidy nests. During our twenty-five years in the East Kimberly Region of Northern West Australia, my husband and I grew bananas. The top of a banana bunch forms a deep 'cup'. This was quickly discovered by the beautiful crimson finches and became a favoured site, with the cups sheltering their untidy nests. Unfortunately snakes also inhabited the bunches and often invaded the nests for the hatchlings, giving whoever picked the bunch quite a fright.

Banana picking and nesting often occurred at the same time. Happily, the finches took to decorating their nests with red thread plucked from my floor mop, when it was hung outside to dry. This made the nest obvious and picking was held off until the hatchlings could call, at which point we could pick the nest up and place it carefully in a nearby bunch. This ensured the adults would hear them answering their call, while allowing us to harvest the bunch.

After all the red thread in the mop was taken, I left out small bundles of wool and embroidery threads in various colours for them to take and use as a bunch 'identifier' and discovered that the crimson finch wouldn't take any other colour but red.

Selecting materials for nests

The notes below are starting points for your design.

Sticks and bark strips Ultrasuede can be cut into suitable strips and shapes for these elements. Pre-cut 1mm (¹⁄₃₂in) Ultrasuede can be wrapped around a plastic knitting needle and painted with PVA glue (I favour Aquadhere). Once it has dried, you can carefully peel it off to give you a curly vine-like structure. Silk chenille and bouclé give a mossy appearance and threads such as pebbly-perle and fine Jap silk cords, stitched and turned out, can become stems or sticks.

Grasses Shreds of raffia, pearl and stranded threads, or linen threads such as those used in book making, make excellent grasses. You can also used real grass. I favour certain grasses native to Australia, such as 'fairy grass'.

Decoration Tiny scraps of shaped Ultrasuede attached with a tiny bead make for great lichen. Groups of French knots and beads also work for moss or lichen.

Nest-building materials

Stitched nests – on-frame

Platform nests are stitched on-frame. The foundations can usually be laid directly onto the background into the nesting area, back stitched into position and then finished as below.

Some platform nests are literally a loosely assembled group of sticks on the branch on which the bird is nesting. In these cases there is no need for a background layer. The initial layer, made of sticks, bark ribbons and grasses in appropriate materials, is stitched into the nest area. In such cases the upper parts of the bird, the head, back and tail are positioned and stitched into place over the proposed nest site and further nest structures are arranged coming from beneath the body of the bird and stitched into place. The breast and belly of the bird are then stitched down. Further nest pieces can now be tucked into and under the initial layers, extending the nest and giving it a dimensional effect.

For other platform types, such as those built in boggy, watery places, it is often necessary to place in position a silk organza nest-shaped element when layering up the background. This gives the nest depth and a point of reflection in the water or between reeds. In many cases it is a matter of experimenting with what you have to hand. For example, over-dyed silk ribbon, stitched, distorted and couched beneath the bird can be made to look like duckweed.

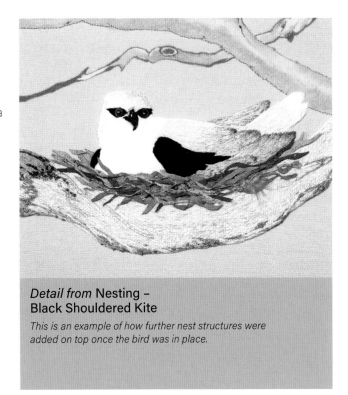

Detail from Nesting –
Black Shouldered Kite
This is an example of how further nest structures were added on top once the bird was in place.

Stitched nests – off-frame

For more three-dimensional nests, you may need to work off-frame. This process is used in *The Nestlings* on page 117.

Preparing the background

As part of creating the background, you need to place an organza nest shape (see detail, right). Where you want to include nestlings (as in the project), add an outline of them too, placed in such a way that the heads will remain visible with the nest in position.

Creating the stitched nest

Trace the nest shape from your Master copy onto calico, then draw in the stitch direction. Stitches for these nests can range from elongated stem stitch to irregular Cretan stitch (either alone or as a combination). Consider using couched soft, thick cottons, silk bouclé or chenille. The main criterion is that the stitching is very close or slightly over-stitched.

After stitching the body of the nest any decorative features can be stitched into place with French knots, beads, downy feathers and/or tiny sections of Ultrasuede representing lichen.

The important feature to note is the texture of the nest. Is it a finely woven delicate grass nest, a solid mud nest or one in between? Is it woven and covered with lichen and moss, as for the rose robins here? Choose the threads and other materials to best suit the nest.

With the stitching complete, treat the nest in the same way as the birds: Vliesofix it and remove the calico, as described on pages 94–95. Place it safely in an envelope until you are ready to stitch it into position.

Stitching the nest into place

The rounded cup-shaped nest can now be traced onto a calico piece and finished as for the bird (see page 94). Applying it to the work, however, is different – see page 117 for the technique.

Detail from *The Nestlings*
This detail shows the organza background shape within the stitched background, ready for the stitched nest to be applied.

Studio folios

This chapter showcases some of many works based on birds and their habitats that I have enjoyed observing, researching and working on over the years. As mentioned earlier, I have lived in three quite diverse areas of Australia. With their differing climates and habitats, the birds can be – and are – quite different from region to region, and each offers a wonderful variety to study and work on.

When we first moved from the banks of the Ord River in the East Kimberley to the New England Region, our new home was perched on the edge of a ravine or small gorge; it was a wonderful place to study and research birds in their many habitats, and many of the birds of this area are represented here.

Now that I live in a town, the variety of small birds that lived around the bush and garden have somewhat diminished. However, I greatly enjoy the birds that have, rather like myself, adjusted to the urban landscape.

Portrait of a Raptor – The Wedge-tailed Eagle

For the birds described in this and the following folios, I have included designs, observations and colour information with the images so that you can, using the information earlier in the book, adapt and use the lessons within your own work.

In the diagrams that follow, the arrows show the stitch direction of the feathers. The first colour mentioned is the thread colour. If there is a '+' symbol, the second thread mentioned is the blending colour (e.g. 844 + 310).

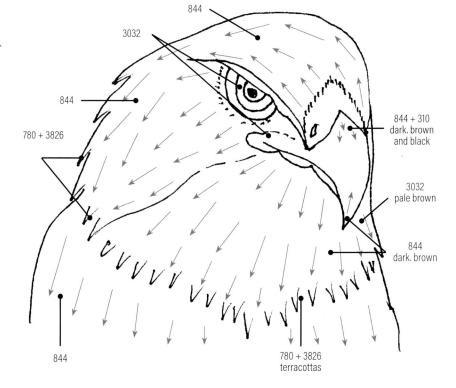

The planned stitch direction and DMC thread colours are noted here.

Portrait of a Raptor – The Wedge-tailed Eagle
12.5 x 12.5cm (5 x 5in)

Initial drawing
As a bold, simple portrait, the initial drawing was a chance to work out the composition.

Courting Colours – The Superb Blue Fairy Wrens

The master copy is presented here at half its actual size. You can scan or photocopy it and enlarge it by 200 per cent for the actual size. Alternatively, you can download and print a full-size copy from Bookmarkedhub.com for free.

   In addition to the general notes on the diagrams (see page 128), the diagram below shows blending. On the wing section the colours are blended as for the stitching of the base; colour progressions are shown as 3032 > 3790 > 3787. Further shading can be added if needed.

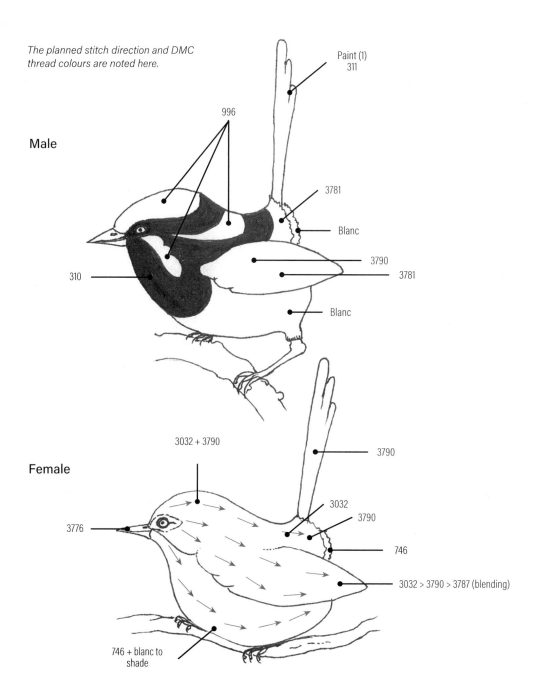

The planned stitch direction and DMC thread colours are noted here.

Male

996

Paint (1)
311

3781

Blanc

3790

3781

310

Blanc

Female

3032 + 3790

3790

3032

3790

746

3776

3032 > 3790 > 3787 (blending)

746 + blanc to
shade

Master copy

Courting Colours
26 x 19cm (10¼ x 7½in)

Dawn Light – Superb Blue Fairy Wren Fledglings

The master copy is presented here at half its actual size. You can scan or photocopy it and enlarge it by 200 per cent for the actual size. Alternatively, you can download and print a full-size copy from Bookmarkedhub.com for free.

STUDIO FOLIOS

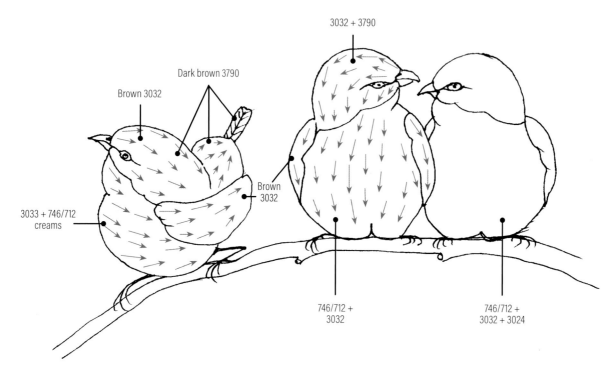

The planned stitch direction and DMC thread colours are noted here.

Master copy

Dawn Light – Superb Blue Fairy Wren Fledglings
31 x 18cm (12¼ x 7⅛in)

Nesting – Black Shouldered Kite

The master copy is presented here at half its actual size. You can scan or photocopy it and enlarge it by 200 per cent for the actual size. Alternatively, you can download and print a full-size copy from Bookmarkedhub.com for free.

The planned stitch direction and DMC thread colours are noted here.

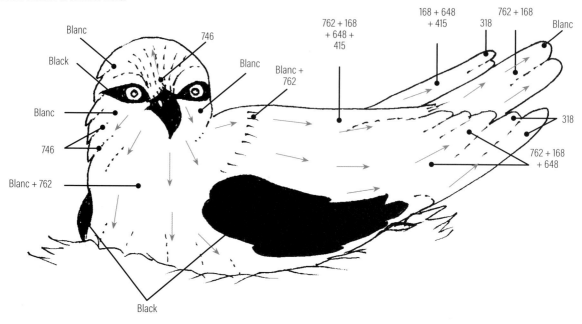

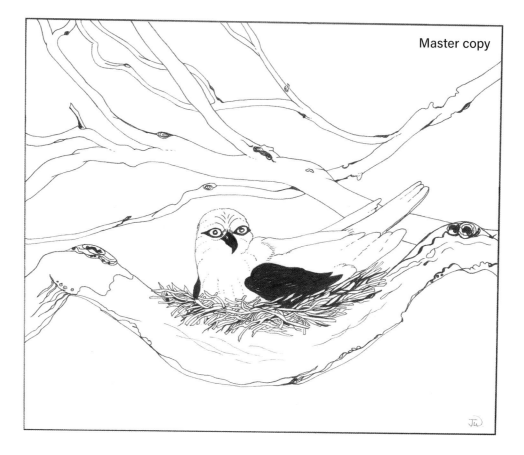

Master copy

Nesting – Black Shouldered Kite

25.5 x 21.5cm (10 x 8½in)

Soft Call of Spring –
The Crested Pigeon

The master copy is presented here at half its actual size. You can scan or photocopy it and enlarge it by 200 per cent for the actual size. Alternatively, you can download and print a full-size copy from Bookmarkedhub.com for free.

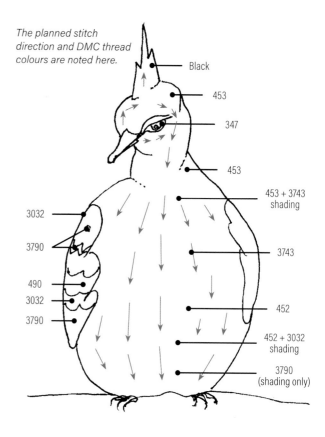

The planned stitch direction and DMC thread colours are noted here.

Black

453

347

453

453 + 3743
shading

3032

3790

490
3032
3790

3743

452

452 + 3032
shading

3790
(shading only)

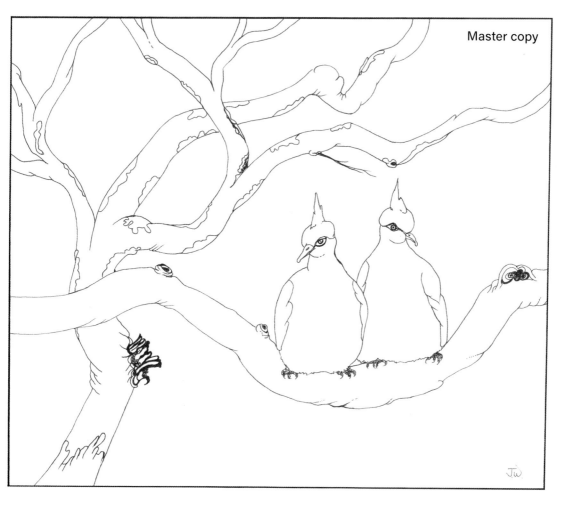

Master copy

Soft Call of Spring – The Crested Pigeon
29.5 x 25cm (11½ x 10in)

Sipping Nectar – The Eastern Spinebill

The master copy is presented here at half its actual size. You can scan or photocopy it and enlarge it by 200 per cent for the actual size. Alternatively, you can download and print a full-size copy from Bookmarkedhub.com for free.

As explained on page 130, this diagram also shows blending, indicated by the '>' symbol.

STUDIO FOLIOS

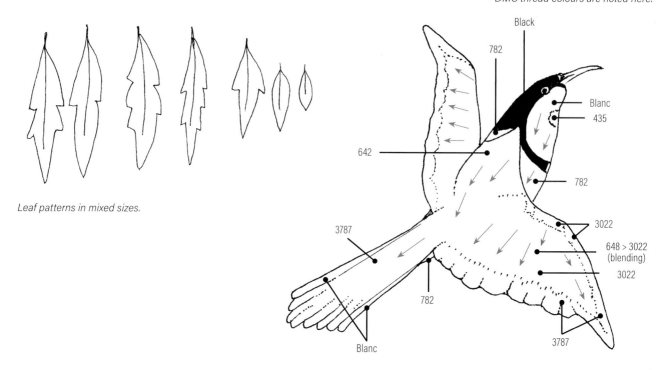

The planned stitch direction and DMC thread colours are noted here.

Leaf patterns in mixed sizes.

Master copy

The flowerheads, marked in red, are made with a mix of French knots and Italian knots (see page 156).

Sipping Nectar – The Eastern Spinebill
20.5 x 18cm (8 x 7⅛in)

On Myall Lake – The Little Pied Cormorant

There is no master copy presented for this piece, as the design is spare and minimal.

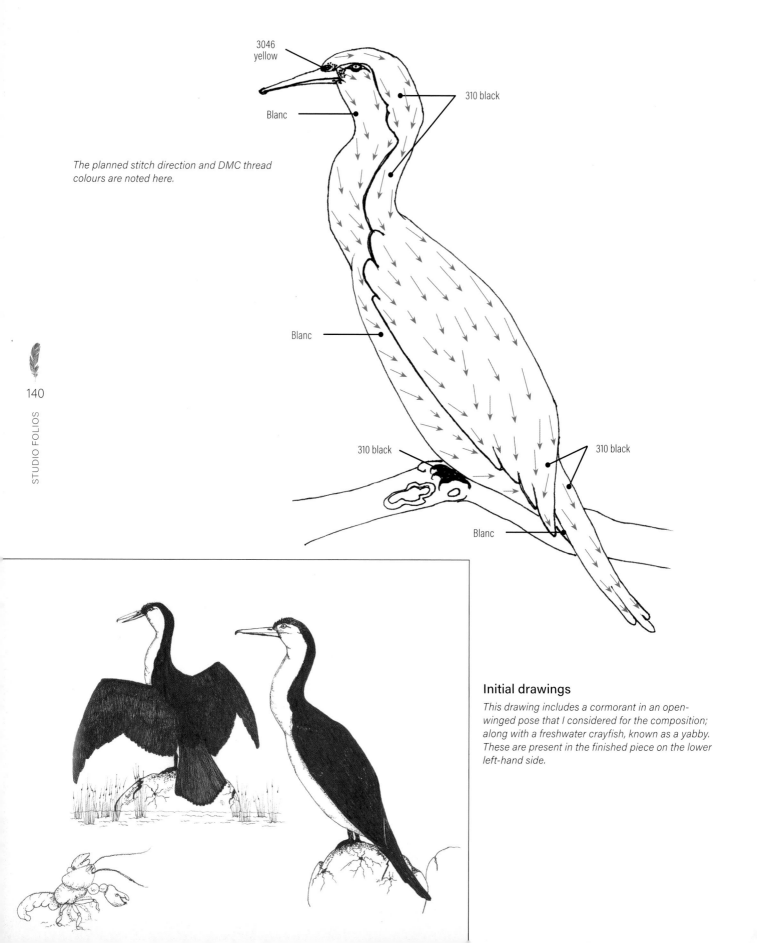

3046
yellow

310 black

Blanc

The planned stitch direction and DMC thread colours are noted here.

Blanc

310 black

310 black

Blanc

Initial drawings

This drawing includes a cormorant in an open-winged pose that I considered for the composition; along with a freshwater crayfish, known as a yabby. These are present in the finished piece on the lower left-hand side.

On Myall Lake – The Little Pied Cormorant

65 x 45cm (25½ x 17¾in)

The yabbies and weed at the lower left-hand corner were made from two fused layers of silk organza, as this creates a firm base from which to cut before positioning under the overlay.

The branches and tree stump were machine-stitched with felt as the base.

Finishing the work

A piece of work upon which you will have spent many hours designing and stitching deserves the same amount of attention when it comes to mounting and finishing. Its presentation reflects not only on the work but on your professional approach, whether it is for a hobby or for an exhibition.

Mounting and framing

I always leave the completed embroidery on its working frame in a place where I can come across it every now and then. Viewing the work from differing angles over a period of time helps me to be sure that there is nothing further to add or change.

A frame need not be expensive or overly ornate. To me, simplicity more often enhances a work than detracts from it. Luckily my husband is a fine wood worker who makes all of my frames in his workshop, I do the mounting, finishing and framing in my workshop. However, most people use a good framer experienced in framing embroideries.

Finishing steps

1 Preparing a board for lacing.
2 Lacing the work to a board.
3 Fusing fabric to a mounting board.
4 Float mounting.
5 Matt boards and framing.

Preparing a board for lacing

The board I use to back the work is a 3mm (⅛in) craft board or MDF (medium density fibreboard) which is sufficiently strong and rigid for the sizes I usually work in. It can be found in craft and hardware shops, and in most cases businesses will cut to size.

Once the work has been removed from the rigid frame re-measure it and have the board cut to this size. This is important because often the measurements decrease slightly when the tension provided by the lacing is relaxed.

Wipe the board clean with a damp cloth, cut a slightly larger piece of polyester/wool felt blend and, using either UHU glue or Aquadhere, glue the felt to the upper surface. Iron the felt to fuse it to the board and, when cool, cut away the excess with a rotary cutter.

Why do I use craft board? Because the work needs to be tightly laced to help remove any puckering that may occur during stitching the work, lacing the work to craft board removes this and helps ensure there are no 'dints', ugly shadows along the edges of the work, as often occurs with foam core.

Removing the work from the embroidery frame

1 Carefully remove the lacing thread and masking tape from the frame. Place the back of the work onto a clean firm surface.

2 Place the 'window' over the work and with a 2H pencil draw around the outside edge of the mounting allowance.

3 Remove the 'window' and trim away any excess fabrics so that only the work and mounting allowance remains.

4 Remove the tacking and isolating stitches and draw any surface threads to the back. Clip all threads off at the edge of the back of the work. Do not iron the work.

5 Fold the excess silk organza at the sides of the work to the front and trim away some of the fabric layers to reduce the bulk. Do not cut away any of the sky or foreground fabrics, and always make sure to leave a layer of firm fabric such as a range, hill or tree line intact, as this will help to stabilize the work and allow a firm pull during tensioning.

6 As you trim the remaining layers, make sure that they are graded so there is no hard edge, which would be difficult to fold over the board.

You will need

MATERIALS FOR LACING

- 3mm (⅛in) craft board
- 2H pencil
- No. 5 crewel needle
- Plastic or glass-headed pins
- Polycotton
- Fabric scissors
- Cotton tapestry warping thread (Bockens Fiskgarn 20/6 is my choice)
- Top-quality PVA glue such as Aquadhere or UHU stick

Materials for lacing

Lacing the work to a board

1 Place the work face down on a clean padded surface and place the prepared board felt side down over the back of the work. The base of the work should show 1mm (1/32in) below the edge of the board, and the edges of the side stitching should just be visible.

2 Using the 2H pencil, draw a wide 'V' shape on the calico backing fabric outwards from each corner of the board (see below). Remove the board and carefully cut away the calico along the drawn lines at each corner. Do not cut away any other fabric.

3 Reposition the board, check the corners are aligned, then cut the calico away on each corner in turn. Fold the top mounting allowance over the board. Pin the mounting allowance into the side edges of the board with plastic- or glass-headed pins, one at each corner.

4 Turn the work and pin the base in the same way, checking that the stitching of the base and sides of the work is visible over the edges of the board.

5 Thread a suitable needle with a long, strong thread such as a cotton tapestry warping thread. Bring it through all the layers of fabric and tie a knot around the layers. Do not tie a knot on the end of the thread, as it is easily pulled through during tensioning.

6 Begin lacing from the left-hand side if you are right-handed, and from the right-hand side if left-handed. Lace the entire sides. Tension the lacing firmly and finish off with two half hitches around the last stitch and remove the pins. Note: with a work larger than 30cm (11¾in), begin lacing from the centre outwards to the edge and repeat in the opposite direction. Tension each side as it is finished.

7 Fold the silk organza back over the front of the work at opposing corners. Very carefully cut away all other fabrics in the corners, using the cut edges of the calico as a guide. Be careful of the stitching of the work at the base corners and never cut into the organza overlay. Fold the organza back into place.

8 The technique of folding in the organza corners is one that I have adapted from book binding. Take hold of the top of the fold and pull it gently out from the work. Without taking your hands away, fold it over to the back. A small pleat will form at the corner. Use your finger to press it into place, then fold the side edge over the back of the work and pin it into place forming a 45-degree angle. Fold the opposite corner and pin into place, then fold the base corners.

9 After folding and pinning each corner, lace the second sides together, beginning at the base of the work. Tension the base area of the work very firmly up to above the top line of back stitching, then ease off slightly over the sky area and finish as before. Remove the pins.

10 Stitching the folds at the corners will further tension the work and help it to lie flat. Thread a no. 5 crewel needle with a polycotton, knot the end, insert and bring up at the point of the corner. Use the needle to smooth under any extra folds into the organza and carefully stitch along the angle towards the centre of the board. Make sure the fabric does not form a 'nipple' on the corner, as they are hard to remove.

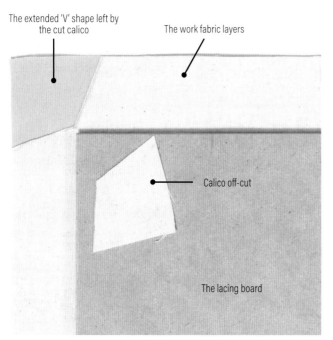

The extended 'V' shape left by the cut calico

The work fabric layers

Calico off-cut

The lacing board

Removing the calico from the corners of the work prior to lacing the work to a backing board. Note that fabric is only removed from the corner, as shown above.

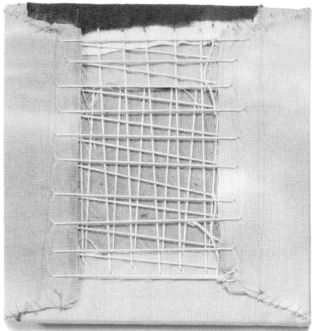

The back of the work after lacing

Fusing fabric to a mount board

Choose the type and colour of the fabric you want to use. This will depend on how the work is to be presented. Generally, for smaller works which have a matt board, I use a white cotton or cream fabric. For larger works, or those that have a design element overhanging the edge of the work, I use a cream seedy silk.

Cut the fabric a little larger than the board, using a craft knife. The thickness of the board will again depend on the size of the work.

1 Cut the craft board 1–2mm (1⁄16in) smaller that the rebate measurement of the frame (see page 197). Clean the board and place it face-up on a protected surface. Iron any creases from the fabric.

2 Cover the surface of the board with glue (or use a glue stick). Allow the glue to dry slightly; wait until the sheen has slightly faded from the glue surface.

3 Place the fabric over the board and lightly smooth it to remove any air bubbles that may form: work from the centre of the board out to the edges. Allow it to dry completely or until the board feels warm to the touch.

4 Iron to fuse the fabric to the board. Trim the fabric from the edges with a rotary cutter when cool.

Float mounting

All of my embroidered works are float-mounted and the matt boards windows are all cut so there is a small margin between them and the work. This is to prevent any shadows falling across the work.

1 Place the work into position on the prepared mount board. Measure the top and sides, making sure they are the same distance from the mount board's edges. Insert three pins into one lower and the top upper corners to indicate the work's placement. I prefer to have deeper base measurement than the top and side for all size and format works.

2 Turn the work over and apply approximately half a teaspoon of quick-drying glue to the back, 2–3cm (3⁄4–1¼in) in from each corner, and a little less glue at the sides at the same distance between the edge of the work and the lacing. This is to prevent the glue from bleeding into the mount board.

3 Turn the work over and place it on the mount board so that the top corners and the base's corner approximate the pin positions. Measure the top and sides again to be sure that they are all the same. If not, carefully adjust as needed. It is important that the measurements are correct, particularly if a matt board is to be used.

4 Remove the pins. Place felt pieces on the surface of the work at each corner and at the sides. Place a block of wood onto the felt pads. Place a firm board and weights over the blocks of wood and weigh them down for approximately two hours. Because there are small variations in height due to the fabric layering, make sure the weights across the blocks are equal. To do this, gently try to move the blocks. If they move even slightly, either add more weight or more felt pads, then check again.

5 After removing the weights, cover the work and leave it flat until the glue cures – ideally overnight.

You will need

FUSING FABRIC TO A MOUNT BOARD

- 2–3mm (1⁄16–1⁄8in) craft board
- Your chosen fabric
- 30mm (1¼in) paintbrush
- Top-quality PVA glue such as Aquadhere or UHU stick
- Rotary cutter and board
- Iron and ironing board

FLOAT MOUNTING

- Prepared mount board and the work
- Glass-headed pins
- Small steel ruler
- Quick-drying glue, such as Helmar 450
- Sufficient felt pieces and wood blocks for each glue position
- A firm, rigid board (such as a hard-cover book) to take weights

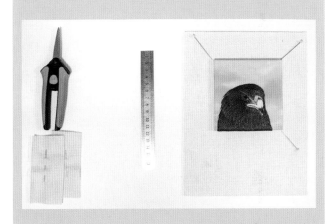

Materials for float mounting

TIP

Don't leave the weights on any longer than necessary: should the work become dented it is very difficult to remove any marks.

Back of the frame

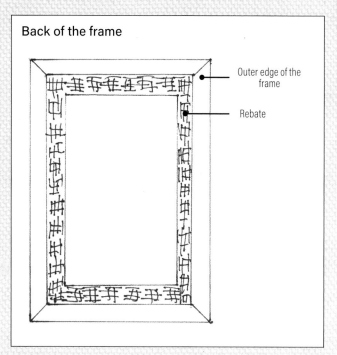

Outer edge of the frame

Rebate

Front of the frame

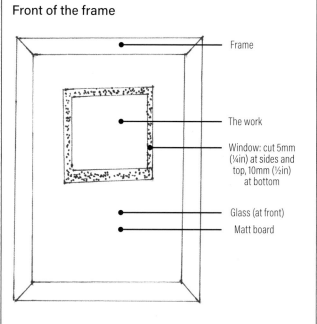

Frame

The work

Window: cut 5mm (¼in) at sides and top, 10mm (½in) at bottom

Glass (at front)

Matt board

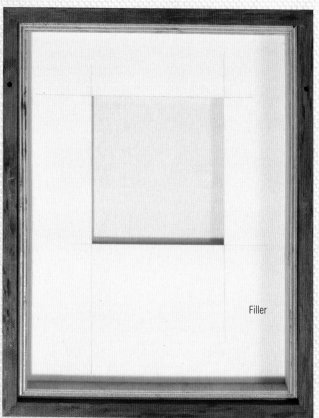

Filler

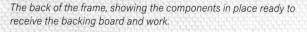

The back of the frame, showing the components in place ready to receive the backing board and work.

Cross-section of the frame

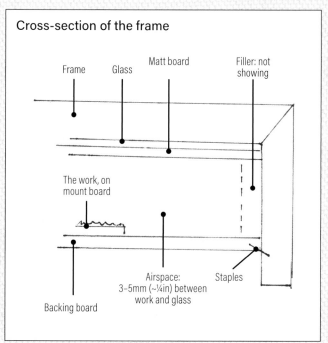

Frame   Glass   Matt board   Filler: not showing

The work, on mount board

Backing board

Airspace: 3–5mm (~¼in) between work and glass

Staples

Matt boards and framing

The frame should be chosen with the aim of enhancing the artwork. It is a personal decision and my choice, regardless of art genre, is always a simple wooden frame made, if possible, with local timber.

The important measurement of the frame is its rebate. This is the recess found on the inside edges of the frame. The rebate holds the glass, matt board, fillers and mount board in position. Should the frame's rebate not have sufficient depth, some framers attach an extra backing. I feel it is better to find a different frame than to do this as I find the piece doesn't lie flat against the wall when hung. This is, however, a personal choice.

The glass used is a 2mm clear glass, cut 1mm (1/32in) from all sides of the rebate. Clear glass is used because it will be standing away from the embroidery. Non-reflective glass will cause the work to appear blurry.

Matt boards are cut as for the glass: 1 mm (1/32in) from all sides of the rebate. The 'window' has a bevelled edge and is cut 5mm (1/4in) larger than the work's dimensions on top and sides and 10mm (1/2in) at the base. Usually I ask a professional framer to cut my matt boards to the sizes I need, mainly because a framer has the materials and equipment to cut windows accurately.

Because float mounting causes the work to stand proud of the mount board's surface, the fillers must be cut to accommodate the height of both and include a small amount of air space between the work and glass. They can be cut from 10mm (1/2in) craft board (MDF) or foam core with mitred corners to keep them firmly in place.

You will need

FRAMING
- Frame
- 2mm (1/16in) clear glass
- Matt board
- Mount board (for float-mounted work)
- Fillers cut to accommodate height of all above and the backing board
- Glass cleaning materials
- Soft cloths
- Stiff and soft brushes
- Staples
- 50mm (2in) gummed paper
- D-rings and hanging wires

Cleaning

Ideally you would have two work surfaces, one for cleaning and one for framing. Clean the matt board and the work with a soft brush to make sure there is no dust or tiny thread scraps on the work. Clean all dust from the frame rebates and fillers with a stiff household brush followed by a damp cloth. Clean the glass with a glass cleaner or similar and paper towelling.

Framing

Framing is my least favourite part of the process. It is time consuming, involves a lot of space, and is often frustrating. Due to this, I usually leave the task until I have a group of works for exhibition or a gallery and do them all together. Once complete, and all the works are lined up, it is very satisfying.

1 Place the frame front down onto a clean surface and place the glass into the frame. Hold it up to the light and check for marks or flecks of dust. If clean, place the matt board over the glass and again check for scratches on the glass, dust and any other marks.

2 Place the fillers into position in the rebates and make a final check before placing the backing board with the mounted work into position. Check again, then staple all together through the backing board into the frame.

3 Paper around the rebate area with the gummed paper and attach D-rings and hanging wire. I attach the rings approximately 50mm (2in) from the top of the frame, as I have found that placing them one third of the frame's side measurement from the top, as often recommended, causes the frame to tilt forward from the wall rather than lying flat.

4 Finally, glue your card on the back – titled, signed and dated if you wish.

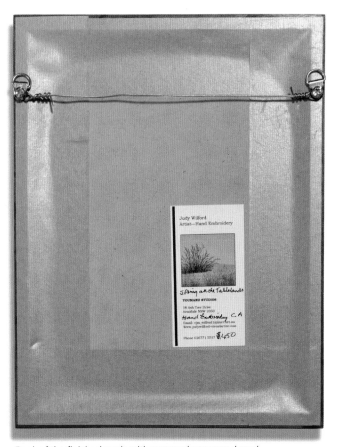

Back of the finished work, with gummed paper and card secured in place.

Master works

The following are some of my past works, revolving around a few of the birds I have observed over the many years spent living in different parts of Australia. Birds and their habitats, and the wonder of flight, have fascinated me since childhood. The works here include images with details, and some include notes that highlight points of interest, or explain the reasons they came to be designed and stitched.

One Small Life in the Scheme of Things – Superb Blue Fairy Wren

This work tells the story of the life of the superb blue fairy wren. It is divided into four main sections. The first shows the overall habitats of the wren in the New England region. The second shows the more intimate habitat and the courting ritual, where the male drops a tiny petal during the ritual 'dance'. The third shows the nesting and nurturing of the young. The nest observed was built in a mass of vine and bracken. Both male and female attend the nest, as well as immature birds from previous nesting. At this time the male's colouring is at a diminishing stage as the season ends. The fourth section shows the young fully fledged and snuggling up on a small horizontal limb in the evening.

The four sections are connected with symbols representing the concepts of male, female, pregnancy, birth and family. The surrounding tiles depict behavioural rituals, associated flora, food and predators.

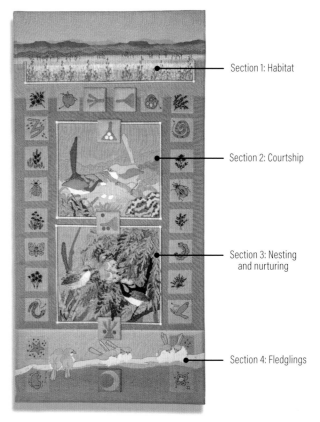

Section 1: Habitat

Section 2: Courtship

Section 3: Nesting and nurturing

Section 4: Fledglings

Opposite:
One Small Life in the Scheme of Things – Superb Blue Fairy Wren
38 x 72cm (15 x 28¼in)

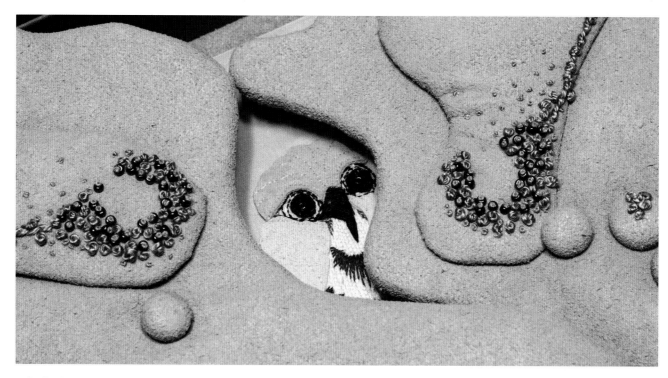

Birds in Boabs

Based on the concept of the protection of birds within the cover of a large tree, this work comprises one large box which contains five smaller boxes, each with a bird embroidered in a variety of appliqué and stitchery techniques. The piece is shown closed to the right, and can be seen open overleaf, on page 152.

The large box is covered in grey Ultrasuede, the colour of the bark of the large baobab tree (known locally as 'boabs') which made up a part of my garden in the Kimberley. The birds depicted are the blue-faced honeyeater, the little corella, the peaceful dove, the whistling kite at the top, and the yellow-faced honeyeater.

This detail of the whistling kite remains visible when the box is closed (see below).

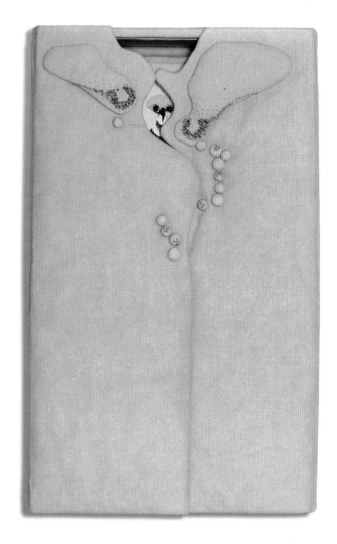

Clockwise from top left: the little corella, blue-faced honeyeater, the peaceful dove, the yellow-faced honeyeater, and the whistling kite.

Birds in Boabs

32 x 75 x 7.5cm (12½ x 29½ x 3in)

Morning Flight – The Forest Raven

Ravens are thought to be among the most intelligent of birds. The inspiration for this piece came from a particular period in my life. Every morning ravens would gather and, taking the same flight pattern, advertise their territory within the forest boundary through a variety of deep guttural calls, with their hackles displayed.

Morning Flight – The Forest Raven
38 x 38cm (15 x 15in)

Stitch glossary

To me stitching is not an exact science. Stitches fill a space and are adjusted in any way necessary to fulfil a function. Stitches are adaptable; they can be regular or irregular, even or uneven, short or elongated, large or small. The beauty of stitching on a rigid frame is that one has complete control of the position and direction of the thread and therefore the stitch.

Basic embroidery stitches

You are likely already familiar with the stitches here. They are the basics that you will need to know for embroidery – and the basis on which the adapted stitches (on pages 158–159) are based.

• ↑ = bring the needle/thread up through the fabric.
• ↓ = take the needle/thread down through the fabric.

> **TIP**
>
> Of all the stitch glossaries I own, the one I have gained most from is the *Encyclopedia of Embroidery Stitches – Including Crewel* by Marion Nichols, published by Dover publications.

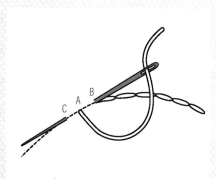

Back stitch

Bring the needle out through the fabric at A, back in at B and out at C. Keep the stitches small and even.

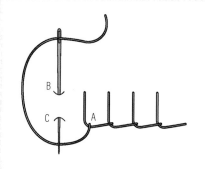

Blanket stitch

Insert the needle where you want the bottom of the stitch to end up (A), then pull it up through the fabric. Take the needle back through at B, above and left of your starting point.

Where you place B will depend on how tall and far apart you want the resulting stitch. Bring the needle back through at C, in line with B.

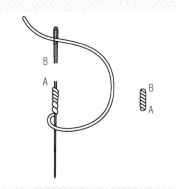

Bullion stitch

Decide on the length of knot required, then calculate the number of wraps required. Using a milliner's needle, bring it up through the fabric at A, then take it down at B, leaving a long loop.

Bring it back up at A and wrap the thread around the needle the required number of times. Holding the wraps between thumb and forefinger of your left hand, pull the needle through with your right hand. Pull firmly and take it down again at B, gently stroking the wraps into place on the surface.

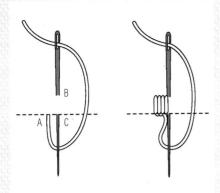

Buttonhole stitch

Sewing from left to right on the line to be worked, bring the needle up at A and down at B, holding the loop of the thread with your left thumb.

Bring the needle up on the line at C, over the loop of thread, then pull it through to form a looped edge.

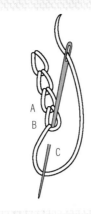

Chain stitch

Bring the needle out at A, then back again through the same hole, holding the loop with your left thumb. Bring the needle up through the loop at B, then draw the thread through.

Take the needle back down inside the loop at B to make a second loop, and bring it up at C.

Repeat this to work a row of chain stitch, and secure it at the end with a small straight stitch.

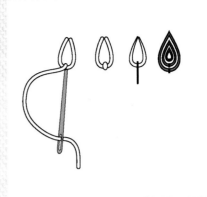

Chain stitch, detached

This is worked in the same way as chain stitch (see left), but each loop is secured with a small straight stitch individually.

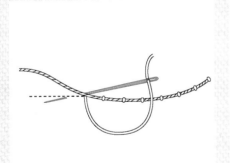

Couching stitch

This is used to attach threads (or a single thread) to a background fabric with vertical stitches worked at regular intervals. Bring the laid thread up from the back to the front, then hold it in place with your thumb while you use a separate working thread to secure it to the fabric.

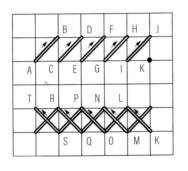

Cross stitch

This stitch is worked in horizontal rows from left to right. Start by bringing up the needle at the lower left hole of one square of fabric (A), and take it down at the upper right hole of the square (B).

Bring your needle back up through the hole directly below (C) and down at the upper right hole of the new square (D). Continue along to the end of the row (J), then bring the needle up in the hole directly below (K) and begin stitching back from right to left.

Make crosses by taking the needle down at L, up at M, down at N, and so forth to the end of the row.

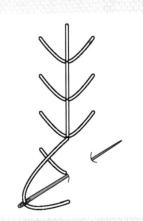

Fern stitch

Each section of this stich is made as a group of three straight stitches, all worked into the same ending hole. The groups are stitched repeatedly, to make a row.

Start by making a diagonal stitch from top left to the lower centre right, then make a second stitch above the ending hole and back to the central hole. Make a third stitch diagonally from the centre to the upper right.

Repeat making this group of three stitches along the marked line on your fabric to the end of the row.

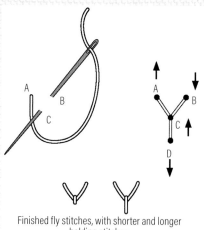

Finished fly stitches, with shorter and longer holding stitches.

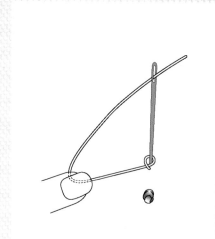

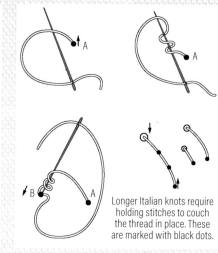

Longer Italian knots require holding stitches to couch the thread in place. These are marked with black dots.

Fly stitch

Bring the thread up at A and down B. Next, bring it up at C. Pull the thread through to form a V, then take the thread down at D and pull through to form the stitch. Bring the thread up in place for the next stitch.

You can vary the length of the holding stitch (C–D) for different effects.

French knot

Bring the needle through, wrap the thread once around the needle, then re-insert the needle into the fabric. Before you pull it through, draw the thread tight around the needle, then take the needle down and through the fabric, holding tight all the time.

To increase the size of the knot, use more strands of thread.

Italian knot

This is a particularly useful stitch for working the stamens of clematis, lilies and so forth. It is worked like a French knot, except that the needle is taken down a short distance from where it came up, rather than at the same point.

Bring the needle up at your start point (A), then wrap the thread around the shaft of the needle two or three times.

Insert the needle at B, where the knot will end. Slide the wraps down to the fabric and pull the thread tight. Holding the wraps in place, pull the needle and thread through.

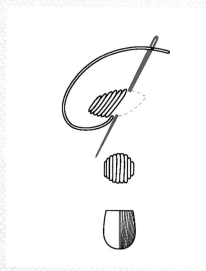

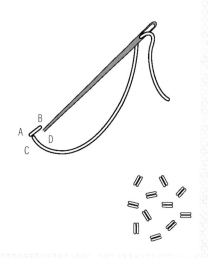

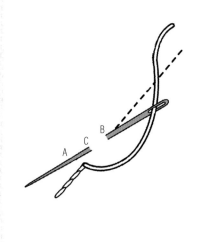

Satin stitch

This is a series of flat filling stitches that are particularly useful when creating leaves or petals. Work horizontal or vertical straight stitches closely together, covering all the fabric. Satin stitch can be worked over a padding of felt, or pad stitches can be used.

Seed stitch

Pairs of straight stitches worked closely together, seed stitches in groups look – as the name suggests – like a sprinkling of seed.

To work a seed stitch, bring the needle up at A and down at B, then up at C and down at D.

Stem stitch

This stitch is a traditional outlining stitch. To work stem stitch, bring your needle up at A, down at B, then up through C.

You can vary the length, which makes it very versatile. When the stitches are worked around 10–15mm (⅜–½in) each – that is, three or four times the length shown above – they can be used for filling the birds. This variation – elongated stem stitch – gives excellent coverage of the base fabric and works well as a filling stitch.

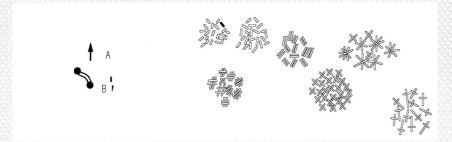

Straight stitch, seeded

This is a filling (texturing) stitch that can be stitched in many forms to form different patterns to fill a space.

Bring the needle up at A and take it down at B in a straight line, bringing it up again ready to start the next stitch.

With control of the stitch, experimentation will allow you to find the patterns you like, or that suit the piece best. Fly stitch, along with and French and Italian knots, can also be used as filling stitches in a similar way.

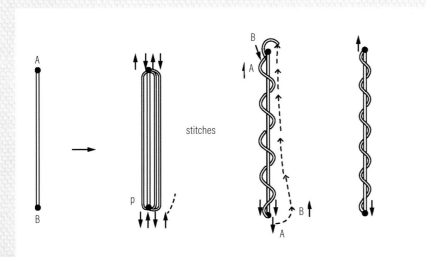

stitches

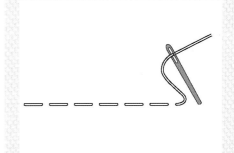

Straight stitch, wrapped

Bring the thread up at the top of the stitch (A), and down where you want the base of the stitch to sit (B), then pull through. Follow this stitching sequence: up at A, down at B, across and up at B, taking the thread down at A, across and down at A, and so forth.

Always work with an odd number of stitches so that the last stitch is taken down at the base. This example has five stitches.

Wrapping When the thread is taken down at the base, it is taken under the surface and brought up at the top, in the middle of or close to the group of stitches. For each wrap, slide the needle under the threads from the right to the left. Make as many wraps as will bind the stitched threads together into one, but do not wrap it so tightly that it appears cord-like.

Gently tug or pull the wrapping thread, mouthing out the wraps. Take the thread down and finish off with a tiny back stitch into the base stitches.

Tacking/basting stitch

A row of long running stitches, often used as a temporary stitch to hold fabric in place until permanently sewn.

Adapted stitches

The stitches here have been adapted from the traditional approach to better suit my work.
The instructions for adapted feather stitch are on page 77. Note the following:

- Always bring the thread up at the top point of the structure to be stitched.
- Always hold the thread in a straight line in the direction of the stitch sequence and stitch close to the required side of the held line and realign the thread after each stitch is taken.

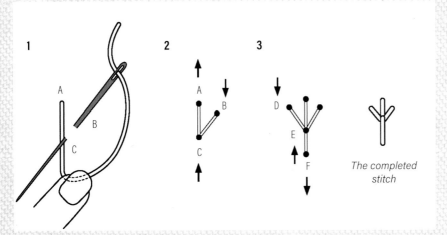

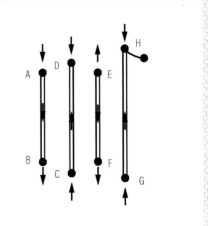

The completed stitch

Adapted fly stitch – 'claw stitch'

The traditional fly stitch is adapted to form a 'claw' upon which a canopy can be stitched, such as a lace flower. This is how the shrubs in *A Brief Flash of Red* (see page 87) are worked. The stitch sequence differs in that the stems are opposite rather than alternating as in the adapted feather stitch on page 77.

1 Bring the thread up at A, take it down at B and bring the thread up below and between A and B at C. Pull through to form a 'V' shape. Take the thread down at D and pull through to form the catch stitch. Bring the thread up in place for the next stitch.

2 To form the first part of the claw, bring the thread up at the top or central position of the structure at A. Take it across to the right and bring it down at B, a little below A. Hold the thread in a straight line and bring it up at C on the right side to make a loop and pull through. Do not make the catch stitch.

3 The 'claw': Take the thread across to the left of the central line, and take it down at D. Bring the thread up at E, on the left side of the first stitch next to C, and pull through. Make the catch stitch to the required length and angle and bring it up into position on the right for the next stitch sequence, following the stitched example.

Adapted laid stitch

This stitch is used for the grasses in *A Brief Flash of Red* (see page 82). The stitched sequence, as shown, is worked across the width of the first grass layer.

The first stitches are 1cm (½in) apart and become straight guide stitches. The gaps are then filled in using the same stitch sequence. This is followed by layer two completed with layer three, and so on.

Adapted twisted chain stitch

This stitch has an open appearance and is suited to many native grasses. It is used for the grass flower spikes in *A Brief Flash of Red*, detailed on page 85.

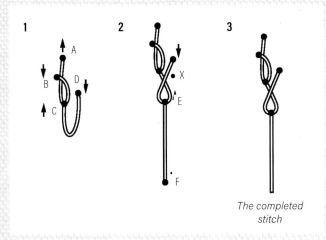

The completed stitch

1 Bring the thread up at the top point A. Take it down at B and pull through the loop at C. Note: the straight top section of the stitch will be approximately the same length as the loop. Do not make the catch stitch.

2 Take the thread across and down at D, then pull through to form a loose loop. Hold the loop and 'flip' it over forming a cross below the first stitch and above the held loop. Bring the needle up in the loop at E and pull through and take a long (catch) stitch down to F at the base line of the work.

3 Note that the grass flower spike is always in line with the catch stitch that forms the stem, regardless of angle or direction. Bring the thread up into position for the next stitch.

Bibliography

These are a few among the many books I have found helpful and inspirational. Some have information and techniques I have used or may use in the future. Some I return to often, others I browse through for the pure enjoyment of the imagery within.

The Field Guide to the Birds of Australia Simpson and Day: Viking O'Neil, 1989

The Complete Book of Australian Birds Readers Digest: Sydney, 1986

Bird Life: An Introduction to the World of Birds AD Cameron and Dr C. Perrins: Elsevier Phaidon Press, 1976

Australian Birds Robin Hill: Thomas Nelson Australia, 1976

Remote & Wild: Seeking the Unknown Australia Richard and Carolyn Green: Fine Focus Press, 2001

Cape Arid Phillipa and Alex Nikulinsky: Fremantle Press, 2012

John Wolseley: Land Marks III Sasha Grishin: Thames and Hudson Australia, 2015

Australian Endangered Species Derrick Ovington: Cassel Australia Ltd., 1978

Australia the Beautiful Wilderness Allan Moult & Leo Meier: Wattle Books, 1983

Australia the Untamed Land Richard Woldendorp: Readers Digest Sydney, 1988

Crossing Over. Where Art and Science Meet Stephen Jay Gould and Rosamond Wolff Purcell: Three Rivers Press, 2000

Design and Form: The Basic Course at the Bauhaus Johannes Itten: Revised Edition: John Wiley & Sons. Brisbane, 1975

The Elements of Design: Rediscovering Colours, Textures, Forms and Shapes Loan Oei, and Cecile De Kegel: Thames & Hudson London, 2002

The Art of Annemieke Mein: Wildlife Artist in Textiles Annemieke Mein: Viking Penguin Books Australia Ltd., 1992

The Art of Embroidery. Inspirational Stitches, Textures and Surfaces Françoise Tellier-Loumagne. Thames and Hudson, 2007

Complex Cloth: A Comprehensive Guide to Surface Design Jane Dunnewold: Martingale & Company, USA. 1996

Encyclopaedia of Embroidery Stitches including Crewel Marion Nichols. Dover Publications New York, 1974

Index

5⊘ SEARCH PRESS LIMITED
The world's finest art and craft books

⫿⫿BOOKMARKED
The Creative Books Hub

from Search Press and David & Charles

WHY JOIN BOOKMARKED?

- Free membership of the world's leading art and craft book community

- Exclusive offers, giveaways and competitions

- Share your makes with the crafting world

- Free projects, videos and downloads

- Meet our amazing authors!

www.bookmarkedhub.com

For all our books and catalogues go to **www.searchpress.com**

www.searchpressusa.com   www.searchpress.com.au

Please note that not all of our books are available in all markets

Follow us @searchpress on:

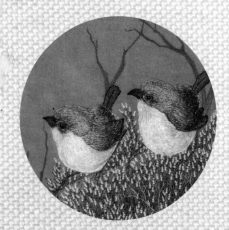